# Where to See Wildlife in
# Tasmania

# Where to See Wildlife in Tasmania

**Dave Watts** and Cathie Plowman

JACANA BOOKS

ALLEN&UNWIN

First published in 2008

Jacana Books, an imprint of
Allen & Unwin
83 Alexander Street
Crows Nest NSW 2065
Australia
Phone:    (61 2) 8425 0100
Fax:       (61 2) 9906 2218
Email:    info@allenandunwin.com
Web:      www.allenandunwin.com

National Library of Australia
Cataloguing-in-Publication entry:
Watts, Dave, 1943- .
Where to see wildlife in Tasmania.

Bibliography.
Includes index.
ISBN 978 1 74175 202 1 (pbk.).

1. Animals - Tasmania - Pictorial works. 2. Zoology -
Tasmania - Pictorial works. 3. Mammals - Tasmania -
Pictorial works. 4. Birds - Tasmania - Pictorial works. 5.
Wilderness areas - Tasmania - Pictorial works. I. Plowman,
Cathie, 1958- . II. Title.

591.9946

Internal design by PinchMe Design
Maps by Ian Faulkner
Set in 9/13 pt ITC Century
Printed in China through Colorcraft Ltd, Hong Kong

10 9 8 7 6 5 4 3 2 1

p. 1: Juvenile Tasmanian Devil.

p. 2: Cormorants roosting at
Narawntapu National Park.

pp. 4–5: Juvenile Common
Wombats.

pp. 12–13: Southern Right Whale
breaching near Bicheno.

pp. 18–19: Juvenile Shy Albatross
on Albatross Island, Bass Strait.

p. 21: Cradle Mountain with
Deciduous Beech in autumn
© Rob Blakers.

p. 47: Forester Kangaroos at
Mt William National Park.

p. 101: The Organ Pipes,
Mt Wellington, Hobart
© Dennis Harding.

p. 167: Giant Grass Tree or
Pandani in Southwest National
Park © Rob Blakers.

# Acknowledgments

Many people have helped with and contributed to the compilation of this guidebook. It is not possible to mention everybody so please accept our apologies if we have unintentionally neglected to include your name.

The Parks and Wildlife Service staff, Tasmania, have always been extremely helpful and kindly allowed us to use their excellent maps as a basic reference for our own. Special thanks must go to Jenni Burdon and Ingrid Albion for reading the text at short notice. Many thanks also to Steve Johnson and Mark Holdsworth for their assistance.

It has been a great pleasure working with Cathie Plowman on the preparation of this book, which would not have been possible without her input.

Special thanks must also go to Jim Napier, Rob Blakers and Dennis Harding, who have kindly allowed us to use some of their superb images.

My sincere thanks, as always, to my wife Helen, who is my greatest supporter. She has been a patient and loving companion on many extended field expeditions and has read the text repeatedly and offered constructive advice where necessary.

Finally a special thanks to Louise Egerton for approaching me with the idea for this book. A big thanks to Angela Handley and the staff at Allen & Unwin for their editorial and design expertise.

**Dave Watts**

Firstly, my thanks to Dave Watts for inviting me to join him in writing this book. It has been my privilege to enjoy the Tasmanian bush and its wildlife for 30 years and it is a joy to share this with others. People who helped me along the way are Vanessa Beckitt, Stewart Blackhall, Tonia Cochrane, Janet Fenton, Michelle Foale, Richard Hale, Janice Miller, Chris Moore, Priscilla Park, Fiona Preston and Linda Riseley. My biggest thanks is for my husband David Butler who patiently supports me in all my endeavours.

**Cathie Plowman**

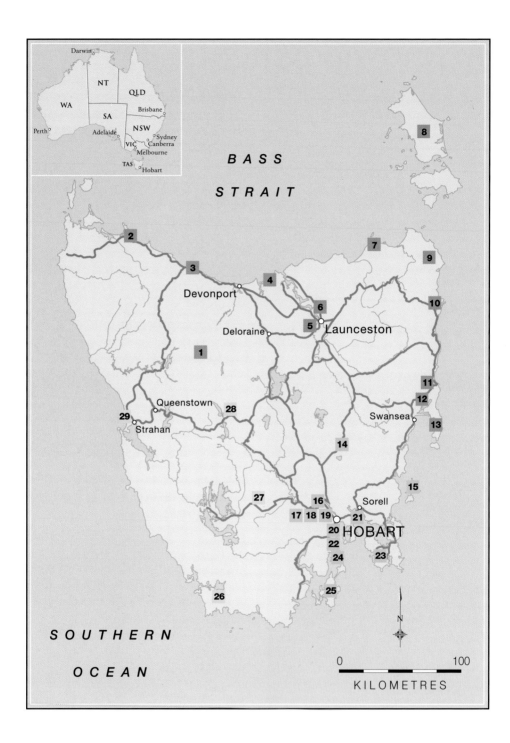

BASS STRAIT

Darwin
NT
QLD
WA
SA
Brisbane
NSW
Adelaide
VIC
Sydney
Canberra
Melbourne
TAS
Hobart
Perth

2

3

Devonport

4

7

9

6

10

5

Launceston

Deloraine

1

11

12

Queenstown

28

Swansea

13

29

Strahan

14

15

27

16

Sorell

17 18 19

21

20 HOBART

22

24

23

25

26

SOUTHERN

OCEAN

N

0    100

KILOMETRES

# Contents

# Introduction

Open plains of the midlands and north-east Tasmania are the favoured habitat of the Forester Kangaroo (above). This large macropod is largely a grazing animal preferring grasses.

The island of Tasmania, located off the south-east corner of Australia, is one of the world's most mountainous islands. With a human population of around 470,000, there remain huge areas of wilderness and wild country still teeming with a diverse range of fascinating and unique wildlife. Where else can you find such an island with over 30 per cent of the land area protected securely within national parks, reserves and World Heritage areas?

of the state is protected by a series of parks and reserves and a World Heritage area.

The midlands and eastern Tasmania are generally lower in altitude and sit in a rain shadow area. Much of the Tasmanian midlands has been cleared for agriculture, although elsewhere large areas of bushland remain uncleared.

That Tasmanian marsupials are still widespread and relatively common within their island home is largely attributed to the absence of the Dingo (which has inhabited the Australian mainland for around 5000 years), and until recently the European Fox.

Tasmania is also a haven for over 200 species of birds, including twelve endemic species, most of which are surprisingly easy to see. Two other iconic but endangered species, the Orange-bellied Parrot and the Swift Parrot, breed only in Tasmania, but spend winter on the Australian mainland. It is because of this wealth of marsupials, diverse bird species and vast areas of untouched mountain wilderness that Tasmania is frequently referred to as the jewel in Australia's crown. Sadly, this jewel has recently been tarnished by the appalling and deliberate introduction of the European Fox.

In previous years wildlife watching was generally thought of as a safari to east Africa to view lions, cheetahs or giraffes, or perhaps a spell in Yellowstone National Park, USA, to see Elk or American Buffalo. However, a recent eco-tourism boom has put Tasmania on the map, and it is now a favoured location for wildlife enthusiasts and bushwalkers of all ages and backgrounds.

Tourism is one of Tasmania's major industries and visitors can expect high standards in a wide range of accommodation, as well as national parks, wildlife parks and camping grounds. You could easily spot some of Tasmania's special birds as you leave Hobart Airport, as Musk Lorikeets and Swift Parrots are frequently seen feeding on flowering eucalypts in the car park.

Sitting in the path of the Roaring Forties, Tasmania receives more than its share of high winds, with the wild coast and mountain ranges of the south-west being battered regularly by blustery storms. It is here in the south-west that over 20 per cent

It is possible to see all twelve of Tasmania's endemic birds (opposite) in a short stay of two or three days, particularly by visiting Bruny Island. If possible, though, we recommend a visit of at least a week and preferably longer. Tasmania's size is very deceptive, particularly when viewed on a map of Australia where this treasure island is dwarfed by its northern neighbour. The Tasmanian countryside is predominantly mountainous or hilly, and the roads are often narrow and winding, so it does take time to travel to the various wildlife sites.

For visitors with limited time, Mt Field National Park, only a little over an hour's drive west of Hobart, offers a taste of the Tasmanian mountains, complete with marsupials and a range of native birds. Expect to see wallabies, pademelons, bandicoots, possums, Platypus and quolls as well as cockatoos, robins, native-hens and honeyeaters.

For visitors based in the north of the state, Cradle Mountain will probably give the best wilderness experience, with plenty of visible wildlife such as wallabies, Tasmanian Devils, wombats, native-hens and cheeky Black Currawongs.

You should soon see plenty of marsupials—especially at several of the sites listed in this book, where many species are surprisingly tame and unafraid of humans. Please do respect these animals and remember that they are wild and usually surrounded by an abundance of natural food. In particular, please do not feed any of the wildlife, as processed human foods can cause severe health problems for many animals. Feeding can also cause some species to become a nuisance, especially when the main visitor season is over.

This book is divided into 29 chapters detailing individual wildlife-spotting sites, with an overview in each chapter of the

This immature Wedge-tailed Eagle differs from the mainland form in having a pale-coloured nape, which will darken with age to a reddish-gold.

major wildlife species found at each. In many ways Tasmania is one big wildlife site, so much of the wildlife may be encountered almost anywhere. To give just a few examples, I have seen a Brown Goshawk while driving up the Southern Outlet at Hobart, watched a pair of Wedge-tailed Eagles while driving through Kingston, south of Hobart, and encountered a Leopard Seal lounging on the beach at Swansea on the east coast.

## Getting there

Tasmania is easily accessed by air from Australia's mainland capital cities. Car ferries regularly operate from Melbourne, and there is no shortage of car hire companies. Car hire is particularly easy these days, although you do generally need to book in advance in the summer months. If visiting for longer than, say, four months, buying a car could be the most economical form of travel.

## Weather

The weather in Tasmania can be quite unpredictable—snow is possible in the mountains at any time of year. Be fully prepared on any outing with strong footwear, plenty of warm and waterproof clothing, adequate food and drink, plus relevant maps. The ultraviolet radiation is particularly severe in Tasmania, so don't forget a wide-brimmed hat and sunscreen.

## Timing your visit

The length of your visit will affect your choice of sites to visit, as will the type of wildlife you wish to see. A greater number

TASMANIA'S TWELVE ENDEMIC BIRDS

- Black Currawong
- Black-headed Honeyeater
- Dusky Robin
- Forty-spotted Pardalote
- Green Rosella
- Scrubtit
- Strong-billed Honeyeater
- Tasmanian Native-Hen
- Tasmanian Scrubwren
- Tasmanian Thornbill
- Yellow-throated Honeyeater
- Yellow Wattlebird

of bird species can be spotted during spring and summer, when summer migrants arrive from mainland Australia for the breeding season. Many birds begin to breed during August, although the main breeding season is usually October to February. Some birds such as Great Cormorants or Swamp Harriers are quite late breeders, not nesting until February.

Summer and early autumn are usually excellent for seeing mammals, as many species such as Tasmanian Devils, Platypus and Common Wombats experience an increase in their populations at this time due to recently weaned juveniles dispersing in large numbers.

Certainly the choice time to see the greatest range of wildlife species would be October to February where possible.

# Wildlife year planner

## JANUARY

Peak period for migratory shorebirds at wader 'hot spots'.

Short-tailed Shearwater chicks hatch; colonies are a hive of activity.

Swift Parrots leave breeding grounds in eastern Tasmania and disperse to western Tasmania.

## FEBRUARY

Orange-bellied Parrots are feeding chicks.

Peak period for shorebirds at wader 'hotspots'.

Little Penguins moulting.

Recently weaned young Platypus leaving burrows.

Forester Kangaroos give birth during February and March.

## MARCH

Orange-bellied Parrots depart breeding grounds in the south-west.

Migratory shorebirds depart to breed in the northern hemisphere.

Tasmanian Devils mate.

Young wombats seen accompanying mother.

## APRIL

Short-tailed Shearwaters depart breeding grounds and head north to the northern Pacific Ocean.

Tasmanian Devils give birth.

## MAY

Cape Barren Geese begin establishing territories.

Spotted-tailed and Eastern Quolls begin mating.

## JUNE

Cape Barren Geese begin breeding.

Common Wombats more often seen above ground during daylight from now and through winter.

Humpback and Southern Right Whales appear now at Freycinet and other east-coast bays.

## JULY

Wedge-tailed Eagles courting in breeding territories.

Echidna mating period.

Peak period for birth of young Tasmanian Pademelons.

Little Pygmy-Possums undergo periods of torpidity during winter.

Peak period for Humpback and Southern Right Whales off the east coast (particularly Freycinet).

## AUGUST

Bush birds (wrens and honeyeaters) begin breeding.

Cape Barren Geese seen with goslings on Maria and Bass Strait Islands.

Possible sightings of Leopard Seals on beaches.

## SEPTEMBER

Swift Parrots and Welcome Swallows return to breeding grounds.

Platypus mating period.

Possible sightings of Leopard Seals on beaches.

## OCTOBER

Short-tailed Shearwaters return to the same burrows they left last April.

Little Penguins incubating.

Orange-bellied Parrots arrive at breeding grounds in the south-west.

Platypus eggs hatching in burrows.

Humpback and Southern Right Whales seen in sheltered bays along the east coast as they return south, often with calves.

## NOVEMBER

Peak period for breeding birds in Tasmania.

Little Penguin eggs hatching.

Wedge-tailed Eagles feeding chicks.

Juvenile Echidnas seen now.

Australian Fur Seal pups being born.

Humpback and Southern Right Whales seen in sheltered bays along the east coast as they return south, often with calves.

## DECEMBER

Recently weaned young Tasmanian Devils and quolls leave their dens and begin to disperse.

Tasmanian Tree Frogs calling (quacking).

Fairy and Little Terns begin breeding.

Little Penguins feeding chicks.

Peak period for breeding birds in Tasmania.

Australian Fur Seal pups being born.

# Conservation

Compared with mainland Australia, Tasmania is very fortunate to have lost few species of wildlife to extinction. The smaller Tasmanian sub-species of the Emu is no longer with us, and the remarkable Tasmanian Tiger or Thylacine has suffered a similar fate. Although large areas of old-growth forest have now been protected, logging remains as controversial as ever, and land-clearing continues unabated in many areas, threatening many species of wildlife including Spotted-tailed Quolls, Wedge-tailed Eagles and White Goshawks.

There are people who still cling to the belief that somewhere in the vast Tasmanian wilderness a few Thylacines hang on. Some will even tell you that 'the authorities' know where Thylacines are alive and well, but are secretly guarding the location. I only wish it were true.

I do believe Thylacines still existed until very recently—perhaps into the 1990s—but now they are no more. During the 1990s, I set out with a small party to search for Thylacines using a series of automatic Super 8 camera systems that were triggered by pressure mats. With a 12-volt car battery, these systems could function for up to three months. We did obtain film of most of Tasmania's wild creatures, including Devils, wombats, wallabies, quolls and a Tiger

Snake that curled up and slept on the pressure mat, using up a whole roll of film! We did not obtain footage of a Thylacine, but neither did we obtain a record of a Forester Kangaroo or a feral cat.

Intriguingly, we interviewed many people who claimed to have seen a Thylacine during the 1980s and '90s. Some are difficult to disbelieve, such as a wildlife biologist, a surgeon and family from Sydney, as well as a biology teacher travelling with a policeman friend at 3.00 pm in an area historically home to Thylacines and with perfect habitat still remaining.

However, at that time Tasmanian Devils were also abundant, and I believe they could easily have finished off any remaining Thylacines by entering their dens and preying on any young Thylacines left behind while the parent female was away hunting.

Unfortunately, Tasmanian Devils are now also in peril, with many suffering from a debilitating and fatal disease called Devil Facial Tumour Disease (DFTD), which has probably slashed the wild population from an estimated 140,000 to approximately 80,000. It is now believed that DFTD is extremely infectious and is being spread by the Devils' biting behaviour, which occurs during mating and when scrapping over a carcass for food.

Tasmanian Devils have quite a short life span—five to six years—and appear very prone to a boom-and-bust life cycle. Ironically, they are decreasing in number

Spotted-tailed Quoll—This nocturnal, opportunistic carnivore feeds on a variety of live prey as well as scavenging on carcasses.

at a time when they could be of help in eradicating Tasmanian wildlife's number-one menace: the European Fox.

There is no doubt a small population of wild foxes exists in Tasmania and that they were almost certainly deliberately introduced by a person or persons unknown. The evidence to date consists of fox prints, fox scats (faeces), at least three road-kill carcasses, and more than 500 reported sightings, of which the Fox Free Tasmania Taskforce considers about 100 to be reliable.

For many years biologists have recognised that foxes have caused tremendous damage to populations of small- and medium-sized mammals as well as many ground-nesting birds on the Australian mainland, resulting in many extinctions. The experience with mainland Australia shows that for most native species, foxes bring nothing but death and destruction. If foxes are able to proliferate in Tasmania, most—if not all—of Tasmania's land mammals will be at risk.

The planned logging of native forests and subsequent conversion to plantations in Tasmania's north-west and north-east is likely to precipitate serious declines of many species such as Spotted-tailed Quolls, Wedge-tailed Eagles and White Goshawks.

Another serious conservation problem involves the firewood industry. In Tasmania each year, more than 700,000 tonnes of firewood are cut—mostly from the old-growth dry eucalypt forests of central and eastern Tasmania. These dry forests usually have a greater diversity of birds and mammals than wetter forests and are poorly represented in reserves or national parks. Many parrots, owls, possums and bats depend on holes in living or dead trees for shelter, nesting and protection from predators. When dead or old trees containing hollows are cut down, these animals lose their homes and perish. It takes over 100 years for large hollows to form in

---

## FOXES AND TASMANIA'S THREATENED SPECIES

If the European Fox becomes established in Tasmania, some of the following unique and already threatened or endangered species would begin to diminish in number and possibly become extinct:

- Eastern Quoll
- Eastern Barred Bandicoot
- Long-nosed Potoroo
- New Holland Mouse
- Little Tern
- Ground Parrot

- Southern Brown Bandicoot
- Tasmanian Bettong
- Long-tailed Mouse
- Hooded Plover
- Fairy Tern
- Spotted Quail-Thrush

Even now, common species such as the Little Penguin (also known as the Fairy Penguin), Tasmanian Native-Hen, all shorebirds, ground-nesting birds, lizards, skinks and frogs would be at risk. It is therefore extremely important to immediately report any fox sightings to the 24-hour Fox Taskforce hotline by phoning 1300 FOX OUT (1300 369 688).

As the chicks of these Orange-bellied Parrots grow they are fed by both adults by regurgitation. The nest hollows may be as high as 25 metres.

eucalypts. The message is simple: do not cut down any tree, living or dead, that contains holes or large hollows.

It would also be irresponsible to ignore the potential effects of climate change and global warming on Tasmania's unique wildlife. Unfortunately, 'global cooking' is happening now and is destined to become much worse. Many parts of south-east Australia have recently experienced their highest December temperatures on record, with raging bush fires devastating many wildlife species. Already, lower rainfall patterns and higher temperatures have caused many Tasmanian wetlands to diminish in size. Some, such as Lake Dulverton, have almost dried up completely.

One of Tasmania's biggest polluters is the forestry industry, whose huge after-logging fires each year produce vast quantities of carbon dioxide, the primary cause of global warming. While air travel is also one of our planet's biggest polluters, eco-tourism does bring special benefits to local economies in Tasmania and worldwide: the fact that people are travelling to see wildlife and wild areas encourages local people to value and protect the wildlife and valuable habitats. Without eco-tourism, much wildlife would be lost forever.

So what can wildlife watchers and conservationists do? We would encourage every person who cares for Tasmania's unique wildlife and wild areas to vote only

for politicians committed to environmentally sound policies, and to support as many conservation organisations as possible.

We believe that the fundamental problem is human overpopulation of our planet, together with the resulting demands our species makes on the natural environment. Many people still need to be convinced of the importance of limiting and managing our population so that we can live in harmony with the other species that share this planet.

Humanity's most precious asset is the diversity of life on Earth. If Tasmania's pristine mountain wilderness and unique, diverse wildlife are to survive another 50 years, we must all make sacrifices. While there is still time, we must all take responsibility for our fellow creatures so that our wildlife is allowed to survive.

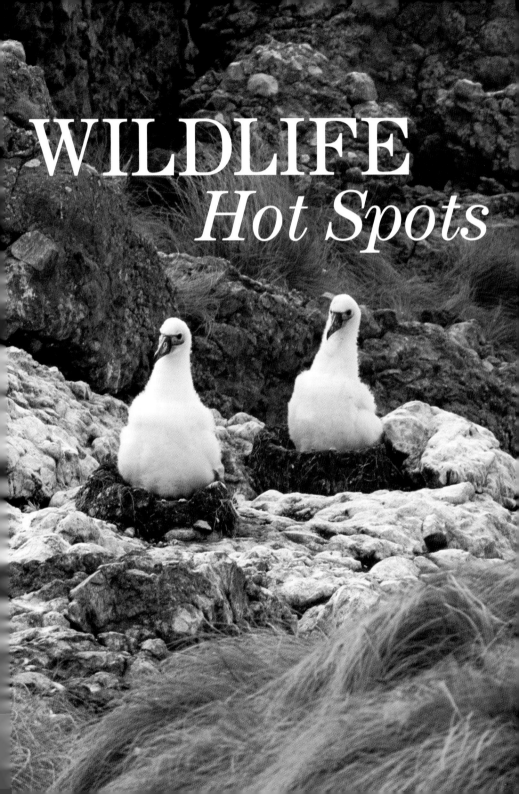

# WILDLIFE
## *Hot Spots*

*The natural world contains an unbelievable diversity, and offers a variety of choices, provided, of course, that we retain some of this world and that we live in the manner that permits us to go out, seek it, find it, and make these choices. We must try to retain as much as possible of what still remains of the unique, rare and beautiful. Tasmania can be a shining beacon ...*

OLEGAS TRUCHANAS 1923–72

# The
# NORTH-WEST

# 1 Cradle Mountain

## KEY SPECIES

- Tasmanian Devil
- Spotted-tailed Quoll
- Eastern Quoll
- Bennett's Wallaby
- Common Wombat
- Black Currawong
- Crescent Honeyeater

For many visitors to Tasmania, Cradle Mountain is high on the list of 'must see' places to visit. Cradle Valley forms the northern tip of Tasmania's most famous national park. Cradle Mountain–Lake St Clair National Park protects 160,000 hectares of vast, pristine mountain wilderness. Here are rugged mountain peaks, glacier-carved cirques, placid lakes and gnarled ancient forests. This picture-postcard symbol of Tasmanian wilderness is inhabited by prolific wildlife, much of which is readily visible.

While the Cradle Mountain area has seen a constant rise in promotion and development during the last two decades, it is still a wonderful place where, despite its high visitor numbers, one can really feel a sense of wild and ancient country and get close to native wildlife.

## Access

Cradle Mountain can be reached in a number of ways. From the north, you can travel from Devonport or Launceston to Sheffield, and then take roads C136 and C132 to the park entrance. It is about a one-hour drive from Sheffield.

Alternatively, Cradle Mountain can be accessed

The endemic Tasmanian Froglet is common in areas over 600 metres. Its call resembles a lamb bleating.

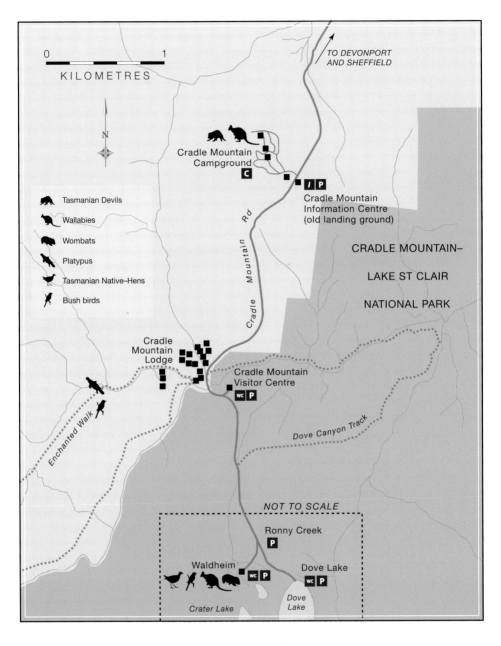

from Queenstown, along the Murchison Highway (A10) and the Belvoir Road (C132). Roads in the Cradle Mountain area can be subject to ice, snow and heavy rain in any month. Roads approaching the national park have been modified to

## Tasmanian Devil
*Sarcophilus harrisii*

This unique, well-known mammal is the world's largest remaining carnivorous marsupial. The size of a small terrier dog, the nocturnal Tasmanian Devil was until recently widespread and common throughout Tasmania. Unfortunately, in recent years a fatal disease called Devil Facial Tumour Disease has decimated populations across Tasmania. It has recently been discovered that tumours are being spread within the population by Devils biting each other during mating and territorial displays. Tasmanian Devils live only five or six years and appear susceptible to a 'boom and bust' life cycle.

The easiest sites to see a Tasmanian Devil are the Narawntapu, Mt William and Cradle Mountain–Lake St Clair National Parks.

reduce driving speeds in a bid to protect wildlife.

There is no public transport to Cradle Mountain, but bushwalker transport services are available. For information and bookings, contact the Tasmanian Visitor Information Network. See the White Pages for contact numbers.

## Facilities

The facilities are spread across a range of locations. Visitors should call into the Cradle Mountain Information Centre, located a few kilometres outside the national park boundary, for a brochure outlining where different facilities are located.

Car parking within the national park is limited and a free shuttle-bus service operates during spring, summer and autumn. Visitors are encouraged to use the shuttle bus, and can combine it with walking sections of the Cradle Valley Boardwalk.

### Information Centre (outside the national park boundary)

Wheelchair-accessible toilets, car park, visitor information, shuttle bus and cafe.

The Cradle Mountain Campground and a range of other privately operated food and accommodation facilities are located within a few kilometres of the national park boundary.

### Inside the national park

Wheelchair-accessible toilets (Lake Dove and Waldheim), walking tracks and cabins (Waldheim).

# Wildlife

There's something different about the Cradle Mountain area that you can sense on arrival: here temperatures are cooler, the air feels cleaner and there's a certain crispness that comes with being in the mountains. Though wildlife is best seen at dawn and dusk, good sightings are possible in the middle of the day.

While a cheeky Black Currawong will probably greet you at the car park (please ignore their pestering for food), the best place to start looking is in the Waldheim and Ronny Creek areas, where adjacent sheltered rainforest and open grasslands provide excellent wildlife habitat. Walking along the boarded track beside Ronny Creek, you'll notice the low ferns and grasses that Common Wombat and Bennett's Wallaby regularly graze. The many animal droppings seen here are indicative of the high levels of mammal activity. Much of the vegetation here looks like it has been ripped up—and it has been, by Common Wombats with their powerful claws.

In open highland areas like Cradle Mountain, Bennett's Wallabies are usually a lighter golden colour, compared with the darker coat this species has in the lower forested areas such as Lake St Clair or Mt Field.

Cradle Valley is one of Australia's premier sites for spotting mammals, with more than twenty species recorded. A quiet walk in the nearby Connells Avenue and Waldheim areas should give you views of Tasmanian Pademelon grazing at the forest edge. A twilight visit to these

# Black Currawong
*Strepera fuliginosa*

This endemic Tasmanian bird is well known as a 'Black Jay' and prefers the wetter and more mountainous areas of the state. It is only during the winter months that flocks wander into the lowlands to forage on farmland or in orchards.

Black Currawongs spend most of the time feeding on the ground, where they are opportunistic feeders on a variety of prey, such as lizards, mice, insects and worms, as well as fruit and scraps from houses or campsites.

At picnic areas or campgrounds in the highlands, Black Currawongs can become particularly bold. They are easy to see at Mt Field and Cradle Mountain–Lake St Clair National Parks.

© Jim Napier

## Crescent Honeyeater
*Phylidonyris pyrrhoptera*

One of the feature sounds of the Tasmanian bush is the loud, metallic 'e-gypt' call of the Crescent Honeyeater. Prior to the breeding season these honeyeaters spread into highland areas throughout the state while some birds remain in lowland areas to breed. As with many Tasmanian passerines (perching birds), the breeding season begins in late winter, when a deep, cup nest is built of bark strips and twigs and placed low in a shrub or tangle of vegetation.

During the winter months, Crescent Honeyeaters move from the highlands into coastal and lowland areas, frequently visiting parks and gardens, especially those with native trees and shrubs.

The long, curved bill of the Crescent Honeyeater is an adaptation for feeding on the nectar of eucalypts, banksias and other native trees. Some insects are also eaten, often being captured in flight.

areas—and onto the plains around Ronny Creek—is highly recommended. Long summer evenings are good for watching small bats as they fly around hawking for insects.

The Cradle Valley Boardwalk is another good location for watching wallabies and wombats. You can see plenty of 'runways', the regular thoroughfares of these animals. Less obvious are the runways and tunnels created by smaller animals such as the Long-nosed Potoroo, Dusky Antechinus (sometimes called a marsupial mouse) and Broad-toothed Mouse. You need to look down low into the scrub to find their tunnels.

To see a Tasmanian Devil, you do generally need to be out after dark. These favourite Tasmanians are regularly seen in the campground, where there's often a den in the breeding season. Unfortunately, Devil Facial Tumour Disease is now common here and the Devils are decreasing in number. If you see a Devil with the disease, please report this to a national parks officer. Wherever you're staying, be sure to wander outside after dark as there is definitely wildlife to be seen—perhaps a Common Brushtail or Ringtail Possum, or an agile Eastern Quoll. The larger and slower-moving Spotted-tailed Quoll is also frequently seen here. Several of the accommodation venues have guided evening tours for viewing wildlife.

A slow after-dark drive along the road into Cradle Valley and perhaps out to Lake Lea (accessed off the Belvoir Road) are other good ways to increase your chances of seeing wildlife. But there are no guarantees, as wildlife is just that: wild.

The Enchanted Walk goes through rainforest along Pencil Pine Creek and, besides birds such as the beautiful male Pink Robin, there are native fish such as the Climbing Galaxias to search for. Find a place where the sunlight allows you to see into the water and have a close look. Platypus have been seen walking overland beside this creek as well as swimming in it. Small tunnels have been constructed for children along this track, and feature paintings to show the wildlife living all around here. Adults will enjoy these as well.

Another resident of the highland pools, lakes and creeks is the Mountain Shrimp, which looks like a short centipede and grows up to 50 mm in length. While restricted to Tasmania, it is widespread in the highlands, so look for it in small pools and at lake edges. This creature is often called a living fossil as it's almost identical to fossils found in rocks that are at least 250 million years old.

Cradle Mountain is the start of the Overland Track to Lake St Clair, and walkers staying in the huts can expect a visit from the endemic Long-tailed Mouse. Its 160 mm tail makes it unlikely to be confused with other species.

With plenty of water in the area, this is also good frog habitat, so listen for some of the six species that have been recorded

## Bassian Thrush
*Zoothera lunulata*

Tasmania's only true thrush is a quiet, secretive bird that spends most of its time foraging on the floor of cool, damp gullies and forests. The Bassian Thrush hops silently along the ground while searching for insects, worms and other invertebrates. The plumage consists of highly attractive brown scallops on a pale breast and a brown back which allows this common but unobtrusive bird to blend well into its environment.

The best sites to see a Bassian Thrush are in damp, shady woodlands at Melaleuca Inlet, Mt Wellington, and Mt Field and Cradle Mountain–Lake St Clair National Parks.

## Green Rosella
*Platycercus caledonicus*

The endemic Green Rosella is common across most of Tasmania, where it is often seen in sometimes noisy flocks. They feed mainly on the fruit and seeds of native trees and shrubs, although they have also developed a taste for cultivated fruit and can be a nuisance in some orchards. Another favourite food is the berries of Hawthorn shrubs, which are commonly grown for hedges in many parts of Tasmania.

Green Rosellas are widely distributed in a range of habitats from the coast to the mountains. They are frequently seen in city parks and gardens, but are also common on most large offshore islands such as Maria, Bruny, Flinders and King.

here, including the Tasmanian Tree Frog. If you hear a 'bleating' call, it's likely to be the Tasmanian Froglet rather than the sheep or goat that concerned walkers often report hearing.

Basking in the sunlight on abundant rocks and fallen logs you'll find little lizards including the Northern Snow Skink and Metallic Skink. Slipping away as you approach, or lazily sun-basking, it is possible to see a Tiger Snake or White-lipped Snake. There's no need to be frightened of them as they'll dash off faster than you.

As with all mountain areas of Tasmania, be sure to scan the skies for Wedge-tailed Eagles, as they are frequently seen soaring above. All but one of Tasmania's endemic birds (the Forty-spotted Pardalote) can be readily found at Cradle Mountain—even around the accommodation areas. Black Currawongs in particular are very common here. While not endemic, the Crescent Honeyeater is one of Tasmania's most widespread birds and you'll soon get to know its call: a loud metallic 'e-gypt'.

A variety of other birds may be seen in the forest including the Green Rosella, Olive Whistler, Scrubtit, Bassian Thrush, and Flame and Pink Robins. On the open moorlands look for Striated Fieldwrens and Southern Emu-Wrens. Ground Parrots also live here—listen for their call: a series of thin, bell-like ascending notes at dusk.

You need little more than patience, warm clothes and sensible shoes to have some really great wildlife experiences in this area. ■

© Dennis Harding

# 2 Stanley and the Nut

As you approach Stanley, the flat-topped Nut rises from the bay. This dramatic landmark is the eroded stump of an ancient volcano, and with the picturesque town of Stanley, which sits nestled beneath it, offers a fascinating mix of history, geology and wildlife. The Nut, the entire town, and many buildings within the town are all listed on the Register of the National Estate. Stanley is also part of the Great Nature Trail, one of Tasmania's official touring routes. A walk to the top of the Nut will offer some wonderful views of Stanley and the surrounding coastline.

## KEY SPECIES

- Short-tailed Shearwater
- Little Penguin
- Peregrine Falcon
- Nankeen Kestrel
- Australasian Gannet
- Stanley Snail

## Access

Stanley can be reached from the Bass Highway (A2), about an hour's drive west of Burnie. The B21 leads from the Bass Highway into Stanley.

Access to the Nut is by a short, steep 10-minute walk up to the plateau, which is encircled by a moderate-grade walk. If you're not keen on steep climbs, you can take the chairlift to the plateau. It operates seven days a week, but is closed from late June to late August.

## Facilities

There are several privately operated tourist facilities in Stanley. Contact the local Tasmanian Visitor Information Network centre for more details.

### The Nut car park

Toilets, café, information on walking tracks to and on the Nut, and a chairlift to the Nut summit (caters for people with a disability). There is a reading room at the top of the chairlift.

A secondary car park is adjacent to the historic Stanley Burial Ground. Wheelchair-accessible toilets, picnic shelter, electric barbecue.

## Wildlife

As most visitors coming to Stanley will be drawn to the Nut, this is a good place to start looking for wildlife. (If you're here in the warmer months, an evening wander will add to wildlife viewing opportunities.) There are varied habitat types on the Nut

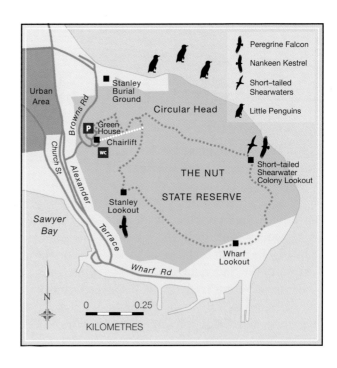

and, over the past decade, there has been a lot of community work to clear the Nut of the invasive weed (gorse) and replant native vegetation. Over 6000 native seedlings have been planted and the native vegetation is recovering well. I've several times seen a Southern Brown Bandicoot come darting out of the bush in broad daylight. Eastern Barred Bandicoots also reside here.

Short-tailed Shearwaters have also been the beneficiaries of rehabilitation work here, with the planting of native grasses enabling the extension of their colony. You can see some of the Shearwater burrows on the plateau walking track itself, and in summer you can regularly hear bird calls coming from the burrows. The time to see Shearwaters is at dusk from late spring until late April (except for a few weeks in November, when both the parent birds are feeding at sea). There are about 18 million Short-tailed Shearwaters resident in Tasmania during the summer months and, as over 13,000 Shearwater burrows have been counted on the Nut, you'll certainly see them if you're here at nightfall. There's more information about these birds and other local wildlife in the reading room at the top of the chairlift.

You have a good chance of spotting a bird of prey here. The Nankeen Kestrel nests on the westward face of the Nut (under the lookout that overlooks Stanley), and this is one of only about ten

## Welcome Swallow
*Hirundo neoxena*

This familiar harbinger of spring is widespread across most of Tasmania and the Bass Strait islands. In Tasmania, this popular bird is almost wholly migratory, with most of the population departing for the mainland at the end of summer. During spring, Welcome Swallows can often be seen shuffling around muddy pool margins to collect mud for their nests, which are built under eaves or the overhangs of verandas and sheds. I have even seen a few pairs nesting under an overhang of a small cliff alongside Lake Dulverton.

Although resembling a Tree Martin, the Welcome Swallow has a long, deeply forked tail, and a dark back and rump.

## Australasian Gannet
*Morus serrator*

This graceful flier is well known for its spectacular fishing technique of plunge-diving head-first into the sea from around 10 metres. Australasian Gannets are frequently seen foraging in small flocks, enabling them to herd fish so as to make them easier to catch.

Australasian Gannets breed on remote and rocky islands such as Black Pyramid, Eddystone Rocks and Pedra Branca off Tasmania, although the bulk of the population breeds around New Zealand.

In Tasmania they are most easily seen from ferries while crossing Bass Strait, on the ferry crossing to Maria Island, and in the D'Entrecasteaux Channel on the crossing to Bruny Island.

pairs that breed on mainland Tasmania. The migratory Swamp Harrier breeds in open, grassy areas on the Nut, and the White Goshawk has been observed roosting on the chairlift cable.

Peregrine Falcons have bred here for many years and nest on the northern and eastern cliffs. These powerful raptors prey mainly on birds and can capture prey larger than themselves, even Black Swans. Their food supplies around the Nut include migratory bird species such as Horsfield's Bronze-Cuckoo, Shining Bronze-Cuckoo, Short-tailed Shearwater, Silvereye, Welcome Swallow and Blue-winged Parrot, which all occur here in spring and summer.

The Nut is an important landing and staging point for these and other migratory birds as they return and depart Tasmania. Even the endangered Orange-bellied Parrot has been recorded here on its migration.

Little Penguins nest on the lower slopes of the seaward side of the Nut, and after dark, the birds can be seen coming ashore here, generally in the warmer months. If you visit in daylight, you'll see some rock penguin 'houses' that were built by a local resident. Little Penguins are very vulnerable to stress from humans, and to attacks from cats and dogs. It's best to stay well away from the beaches at dusk to allow them to come ashore and feed their chicks. A stressed Little Penguin might 'vomit' up the food it's carrying for its chicks before it reaches the nest, leaving the youngsters hungry. If you want to use a torch, cover the light with red

## Nankeen Kestrel
*Falco cenchroides*

This beautiful small falcon is usually found in open country where it hunts—frequently by hovering—for small mammals, insects and lizards. The Nankeen Kestrel does not build a nest, but lays its eggs in a scrape on a cliff ledge, in a hollow tree, or in the old nest of a crow or other raptor.

This falcon is quite rare in Tasmania, but may be seen on the Nut at Stanley. It is also more commonly seen on Flinders and King Island.

© Jim Napier

## Silvereye
*Zosterops lateralis*

A common summer migrant, the Silvereye is one of Tasmania's most familiar birds. It occurs in most habitats including forests, scrub and orchards and is a frequent visitor to shrubberies in gardens, where it feeds on fruit, at bird-tables and nectar feeders. At the end of the breeding season most Silvereyes migrate north, reaching as far as southern Queensland, although some birds do over-winter in the more sheltered and warmer sites in Tasmania.

Tasmanian Silvereyes have a distinctly different plumage to their northern counterparts and are considered to be an endemic sub-species.

cellophane, as the poem on the sign suggests. Please don't shine any torches onto the beach or directly at the penguins.

Shorebirds here on Perkins Bay and Sawyer Bay include the Hooded and Red-capped Plovers, which both breed in summer, and the Double-banded Plover, which over-winters from New Zealand. Both Pied and Sooty Oystercatchers can also be seen on the shores. Seabirds here include the Australasian Gannet, Common Diving-Petrel, and the Little Pied and Little Black Cormorants.

Looking out to sea it's always possible that you might see whales, as several species pass through here on their annual migration. Unfortunately, Sperm Whales, Pilot Whales and Pygmy Right Whales have all stranded and died on the beaches near Stanley. It is thought that the wide, gently sloping beaches here are too shallow to bounce the whales' navigating sounds back to them convincingly.

Historically, Stanley is a very important area, but sadly some of its wildlife has been relegated to history. In 1856 H. Stanley, on seeing a Tasmanian Emu in the grounds of the historic homestead of Highfield, wrote: 'a bird once common on this coast, but now rarely to be met with'. The Tasmanian Emu is now extinct.

You're also unlikely to see the tiny Stanley Snail, even though three populations of this species, which is listed as vulnerable, are known here. ■

# 3 Burnie

Less than two decades ago, the city of Burnie was generally identified with smoke stacks and industrial pollution. But times have changed very quickly and today it is becoming known for restoring, protecting and promoting wildlife habitat.

Burnie offers several wonderful wildlife viewing opportunities: a Little Penguin Observation Centre, a 13 km wildlife circuit that begins and ends at the Little Penguin Observation Centre, and a Platypus-viewing area at Fern Glade Reserve on the Emu River.

## KEY SPECIES

* Platypus
* Long-nosed Potoroo
* Little Penguin
* White-bellied Sea-Eagle
* Tasmanian Native-Hen
* Burnie Burrowing Crayfish

Little Penguins choose a variety of nest sites, including hollows under rocks, burrows dug into sand dunes or scrapes under bushes or even sheds.

## Access

Burnie is located on the Bass Highway (A2), 48 km west of Devonport, and at the northern end of the Murchison Highway (A10). The city is on the Great Nature Trail—one of Tasmania's official touring routes—which extends from Narawntapu National Park just east of Devonport to the settlement of Arthur River on the north-west coast.

### Little Penguin Observation Centre

This is located in Burnie at Parsonage Point, next to West Beach and the central business district. Follow the Bass Highway into the centre of Burnie and stay on the highway until you see the signs.

### The Burnie wildlife walk

This 13 km circuit travels through a variety of habitats in central Burnie. The walk starts and finishes at the Little Penguin Observation Centre.

You can purchase the *Burnie Wildlife Guide*, a guide to the walk and its wildlife, from the Pioneer Village Museum in nearby Little Alexander Street. There are plenty of places where you can join and leave

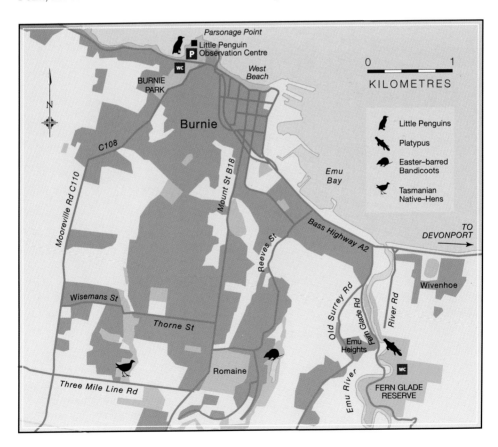

the walk, so you can complete it in stages.

### Fern Glade Reserve

To access this regular Platypus-viewing area, take the Old Surrey Road from the Bass Highway on the eastern approach to Burnie. Turn in to Fern Glade Road. The reserve closes at dusk each day and reopens at 7.30 a.m.

## Facilities

The Little Penguin Observation Centre has a car park, Little Penguin viewing information, and nearby toilets and picnic areas at both the Surf Club and Burnie Park. The Tasmanian Visitor Information Network (with wheelchair-access toilets) is located adjacent to the observation centre.

Fern Glade Reserve has toilets, picnic areas and fireplaces (BYO firewood).

## Wildlife

The fascinating Little Penguins, also known as Fairy Penguins, can be seen in many places along Tasmania's north and east coasts. At Burnie's carefully designed Little Penguin Observation Centre you can actually see what's going on inside a burrow—day or night, at any time of the year. The observation centre is open 24 hours a day and admission is free.

The centre provides in-house accommodation for up to five Little Penguin families, and mirrored windows allow people to view inside the burrows.

## Long-nosed Potoroo
*Potorous tridactylus*

This small, solidly built wallaby with a short, white-tipped tail is widespread in most types of Tasmanian forest as well as heathland. The Long-nosed Potoroo forms a network of tunnels and runways through dense ground cover.

Potoroos dig small holes in the ground surface similar to bandicoots in their search for roots, tubers, insects and fungi. They may be seen by spotlighting at many sites in Tasmania, particularly in areas of dense vegetation.

Of course, as the birds come and go at will, there's no guarantee that anyone will be at home. Little Penguins do come ashore all year round, but their activity is greatest in spring, summer and early autumn.

For the best chance to see Little Penguins here, visit after dark and remain very quietly on the 'human' side of the fence. Do not use torches or flash cameras as these can 'stun' a Little Penguin's eyes, leaving the penguins temporarily blinded and vulnerable to predation by cats and dogs.

Please do not bring your dog to the site, as its scent might attract other unsupervised dogs that might stress or attack the Little Penguins. Life certainly is not easy for wildlife when home is a big city!

The Burnie wildlife walk travels through a range of habitats, offering opportunities to see a number of species. It's probably best to peruse the *Burnie Wildlife Guide* to match up your time and interests with the walk. You might see Masked Lapwings and Swamp Harriers at the old tip site (which is now being rehabilitated), a wetlands area with several species of frog in Thorne Street, Tasmanian Native-Hens along the Three Mile Line, and a swamp habitat of the Burnie Burrowing Crayfish, a species that is now very limited in numbers due to previous hunting. The Burnie Burrowing Crayfish is officially listed as vulnerable, but it is hoped that

## Platypus
*Ornithorhynchus anatinus*

Fascinating and instantly recognisable, this aquatic monotreme is common in most freshwater bodies from sea level to alpine areas. However, this unique creature is easily missed due to its small size and the fact that, even when on the surface, it floats low in the water.

Platypus are most easily seen during late summer or early autumn, when local populations are boosted by the addition of recently weaned juveniles. These juveniles, recently emerged from their burrows, are quite playful, and water levels are generally lower at this time of year.

with protection, education and increased habitat, its populations will stabilise and perhaps increase.

Native fish such as Spotted Galaxias live in Romaine Pond, and Platypus have often been seen here. Romaine Reserve is a good place for a late evening wander when you might see the Eastern Barred Bandicoot or Long-nosed Potoroo, both of which reside here.

The Fern Glade Reserve has pleasant walking and picnic areas, with plenty of opportunities for quietly viewing bird life. Platypus are regularly observed from several places on the walking track including the lower picnic area, the platform midway along the walking track, and at the far upstream end of the Fern Glade (near the Platypus sculpture). As always when hoping to see these animals, quietness and patience are essential.

If you happen to be driving west from Burnie, White-bellied Sea-Eagles are often seen soaring above the coast in the Somerset area.

While you might not have picked Burnie as a wildlife capital, it's a great example of a city where wildlife protection is rated very highly and the local community actively works to protect wildlife habitat. ■

## White-bellied Sea-Eagle
*Haliaeetus leucogaster*

This spectacular bird of prey is frequently seen soaring in graceful flight with typical upswept wings. It has huge, powerful talons and takes a variety of prey such as fish, waterfowl, sea snakes and rabbits as well as carrion.

White-bellied Sea-Eagles are fairly common around Tasmania's coastline, but also inhabit inland lakes and large rivers. They are regularly seen patrolling at several of the sites in this book including Narawntapu, Mt William, Freycinet, Maria Island and South Bruny National Parks, as well as Macquarie Harbour and the Tamar River.

# 4 Narawntapu National Park

This delightful coastal park has been referred to as the Serengeti of Tasmania. Perhaps the description is slightly fanciful, but I do remember sitting on a small hill overlooking the former historic farm of Springlawn late one afternoon and counting 93 wombats grazing! Certainly, Narawntapu National Park is one of the premier areas in Tasmania for seeing a wide range of abundant wildlife.

Narawntapu National Park, which extends to nearly 4300 hectares, was previously called Asbestos Range National Park. Narawntapu occupies a strategic location on the state's north coast between Port Sorell and Greens Beach, on the west side of Port Dalrymple.

Young joey Forester Kangaroos begin leaving the pouch at about nine months of age but continue to suckle until approximately eighteen months old.

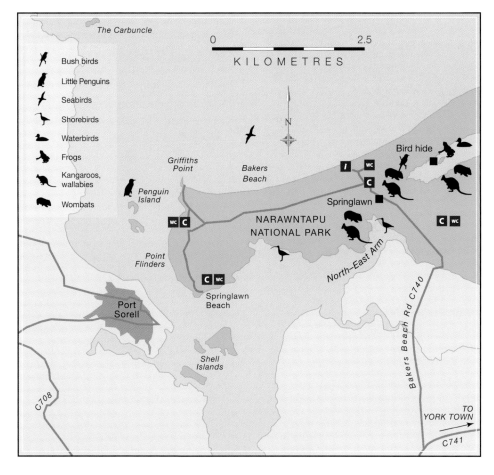

Most young Tasmanian Devils begin to wander outside the den during November and are fully weaned and independent by the end of January.

## Richard's Pipit
*Anthus novaeseelandiae*

This ground-loving, common native is widespread throughout Australia and New Zealand wherever suitable habitat is found. It prefers open grassy areas, stony plains and pastures, and avoids scrub, woodlands or farm crops. Richard's Pipits are frequently seen running across the ground, stopping every so often to snatch a grasshopper, caterpillar, beetle or other insect, while often flicking their tail up and down in typical wagtail fashion.

Richard's Pipit is strikingly similar to the introduced Skylark, with which it is often confused, although pipits are more closely related to wagtails than larks.

The park comprises a wide range of natural habitats including small islands and mudflats in the estuary of Port Sorell, sandy beaches, a large freshwater lagoon, coastal heathland and dunes, dry sclerophyll woodland and the grazing lawns of the former property Springlawn.

## Access

About an hour's drive north-west of Launceston, the park may be accessed via three roads. The major western area of the park, including Bakers Beach and the Springlawn area, is reached from the Port Sorell to Frankford road (B71) west of Devonport. The park turnoff is located approximately 300 metres east of the road bridge over the Franklin Rivulet, which flows north into Port Sorell. From this turnoff a sealed (C740) road extends for 15 km to the national park entrance.

To reach the far eastern side of the park, take the unsealed road (A7) from York Town north to Kelso and on to Greens Beach. A third (unsealed) road allows access to the eastern side of Badger Head. This may be reached by turning left 1 km north of York Town. York Town is about 7 km north-west of Beaconsfield, about half way to Kelso, on the west arm of Port Dalrymple.

## Facilities

Accommodation is limited to three camping areas with basic toilets, fireplaces and picnic tables at the main western area of the park. Camping is also available at the horse yards. Electric barbecues are also available at Springlawn camp area only.

Park staff are normally based in the park during the summer months, and a small visitor centre provides information on walking tracks and local wildlife. An excellent map is available covering the whole park.

There is also a boardwalk leading to a bird hide overlooking the lagoon.

## Wildlife

Narawntapu is largely known as a park where plentiful grazing marsupials may be seen. As usual, early morning and late afternoon or dusk are the best times to watch these mainly nocturnal creatures.

The Springlawn area is home to some of the densest populations of Bennett's Wallaby, Tasmanian Pademelon and Common Wombat known in Tasmania. Many decades of farming at Springlawn have created a lawn-like environment. This habitat of grassy areas surrounded by scrub and woodland is ideal for grazing marsupials. Common Wombats are easily seen throughout the park, often during daylight hours—lack of persecution has no doubt encouraged the wombats to become more confident and less nocturnal in their habits. Bennett's Wallabies and Tasmanian Pademelons are also openly seen near campgrounds. They do, however, normally rest under bushes in dense scrub during daylight hours.

Narawntapu is also a prime site for Forester Kangaroos, Tasmania's largest macropod. Forester Kangaroos originally occurred here prior to white settlement

## Blue-billed Duck
*Oxyura australis*

The Blue-billed Duck is a small- to medium-sized diving duck that prefers freshwater swamps with deep water and dense vegetation. This secretive duck dives frequently and is usually seen singly or in pairs. The male has a rich chestnut body with a black head and pale blue bill. The stiff black tail either drags in the water or is held up perkily.

The Blue-billed Duck may be seen at the lagoon in Narawntapu National Park, the Rostrevor Lagoon (about 1 km north of Triabunna on the east coast), or Lake Dulverton when flooded.

43

but were wiped out during the nineteenth century. They were reintroduced during 1975, and are usually to be seen grazing in the Springlawn area or in the old paddocks surrounding the lagoon.

At the time of writing, Tasmanian Devils are still common here. Narawntapu has remained one of the last bastions in eastern and northern Tasmania still free of the fatal Devil Facial Tumour Disease, and is therefore a great place to catch a glimpse of Devils in the wild.

White-footed Dunnarts are also common, but extremely difficult to see—try spot-lighting after dark along Sheepwash Creek. Brush-tailed Possums are plentiful and may be seen at dusk in the vicinity of campgrounds. Long-nosed Potoroos are found throughout the park, but tend to favour the more dense areas of scrub or understorey and are only rarely seen during daylight hours.

The Port Sorell estuary is a very important area for wildlife due to its large areas of mud flats and small rocky islands. A walk along the estuary foreshore at low tide should reveal thousands of Soldier Crabs scurrying across the mud. These provide a feast for myriad shore birds such as the Pacific and Kelp Gulls, Pied and Sooty Oystercatchers (the latter species nests on the rocky islands), Red-capped Plover, White-faced Heron, Large Black and Black-faced Cormorants, Black Swan, Australian Pelican, Australian Shelduck, and Caspian and Crested Terns. White-bellied Sea-Eagles patrol overhead and Little Penguins breed on the islands.

## Tasmanian Native-Hen
### Gallinula mortierii

This plump, olive-coloured bird is now restricted to Tasmania, where it is common.

These flightless hens can run extremely quickly and also swim well. They prefer swampy, grassy areas mixed with dense tussocks and patches of scrub for cover, frequently near a lagoon, river or farm dam. The nest is usually a cup, formed in a tussock of reeds close to water. As with the Purple Swamphen, a nursery nest is built for the chicks, which are mainly brooded at night.

The shoreline of North-East Arm is an excellent area from which to view the bird life.

Bakers and Badger Beaches are worth checking for roosting Crested Terns, Hooded Plovers or soaring Sea-Eagles.

The large freshwater lagoon was formerly drained for farming purposes, but the outlet has since been blocked, allowing the area to re-flood. This lagoon now provides magnificent habitat for a variety of waterbirds such as the Black Swan, Australian Shoveler, Black Duck, Chestnut and Grey Teals, and Australasian and Hoary-headed Grebes. That bizarre diving duck, the Musk Duck, loves the deep water here, and this lagoon is also one of the few wetlands in Tasmania where the Blue-billed Duck may be seen regularly. Try searching along the heavily vegetated north-western bank.

The scrub between the lagoon and the beach also holds many bush birds, such as Dusky, Scarlet and Flame Robins, the Green Rosella and Grey Fantail.

The woodlands surrounding the campgrounds contain Tree Martins and European Greenfinches; Australian Hobbies are also frequently seen hawking for insects, particularly at dusk. The Tasmanian Native-Hen and Masked Lapwing may be seen in the open grassy areas. This park is a regular site for Blue-winged Parrots, which are sometimes mistaken for Orange-bellied Parrots, which have not been recorded here.

Other commonly seen land birds include the Swamp Harrier, Brown Falcon, Australian Hobby, Green Rosella,

## Common Wombat
*Vombatus ursinus*

Once referred to as a badger, the Common Wombat is in fact a large tank-like marsupial that is in no way related to a badger, which is a northern hemisphere carnivore.

Adult female wombats have a backward-opening pouch that allows the young wombat to graze out the back while the mother grazes at the front. Although the pouch contains two teats, usually only one young is born, and it remains in the pouch for approximately six months.

Common Wombats are most easily seen at Narawntapu, Mt William and Cradle Mountain–Lake St Clair National Parks.

## Grey Butcherbird
*Cracticus torquatus*

Like other butcherbirds, this carnivore hunts by perching quietly on a branch or stump before dropping to the ground to snatch its prey, or even by giving chase through the woodland. Although its diet consists primarily of insects, it also eats reptiles, small mammals, small birds and nestlings, together with some seeds and fruit.

The Grey Butcherbird is well known for its glorious song, which consists of a series of rich and powerful piping whistles, often sung as a duet, and audible over a great distance. It is somewhat solitary except when breeding, when established pairs settle into territories and build a nest, often at the same site year after year.

It is common across most of Tasmania, except in the far west.

Swift Parrot (spring and early summer only), Pallid and Fan-tailed Cuckoos, Horsfield's Bronze-Cuckoo, Southern Boobook, Tawny Frogmouth, White-throated Needletail, Laughing Kooka-burra, Superb Fairy-Wren, Spotted and Striated Pardalotes, Brown, Tasmanian and Yellow-rumped Thornbills, Yellow Wattlebird, Flame and Scarlet Robins, Satin Flycatcher (summer only), Dusky Woodswallow (summer only), Grey Butcherbird, Skylark, Welcome Swallow (summer only) and Richard's Pipit.

A walk to Archers Knob should produce Yellow-tailed Black-Cockatoo, Yellow Wattlebird and perhaps a Wedge-tailed Eagle soaring high overhead.

Finally, some large areas of coastal heathland are also present, and this valuable habitat is home to the elusive Ground Parrot. Several honeyeaters occur as well, including Yellow-throated and Crescent Honeyeaters, with the Tawny-crowned Honeyeater on rare occasions.

As Tiger Snakes are common in Narawntapu National Park, walkers should remain vigilant in all areas, but especially in the vicinity of the lagoon.

Several species of frog have been recorded in the park, including the Green and Gold Frog and Spotted Marsh Frog.

This park has something to offer in all seasons, although spring and summer will yield the most species. Much of the lagoon surrounds (except the north-western side) are bare and unvegetated, being former paddocks. Establishing areas of native reeds or rushes would encourage a greater diversity of birds and amphibians. ∎

# The NORTH-EAST

# 5 Cataract Gorge

## KEY SPECIES

- Common Brushtail Possum
- Bennett's Wallaby
- Tasmanian Pademelon
- Shining Bronze-Cuckoo
- Tawny Frogmouth
- Spotted Pardalote
- Yellow-throated Honeyeater
- Golden Whistler
- Black-faced Cuckoo-Shrike

Cataract Gorge is perhaps the most well-known site in the city of Launceston, and among the most visited places in Tasmania. While some nature lovers might write off the Gorge as being 'too developed' with its cultivated gardens, peacocks and people jogging by, the site is a real gem for birdwatchers: it has one of the state's richest concentrations of bird life, with over 60 species having been recorded.

The Gorge grounds are spacious and relaxing, with plenty of seats and walking tracks, so plan for an unhurried visit. The grounds are open around the clock, making it a wonderful place for after-dark nature prowls.

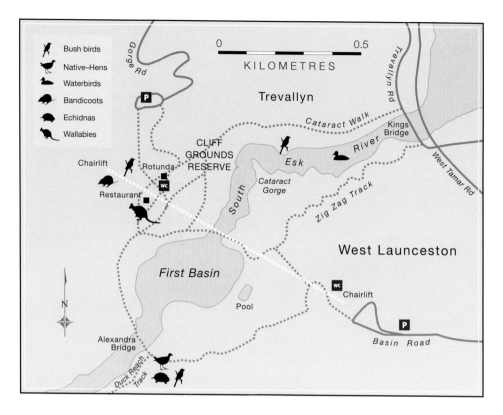

Bush birds
Native–Hens
Waterbirds
Bandicoots
Echidnas
Wallabies

0        0.5

KILOMETRES

Gorge Rd

Trevallyn Rd

Trevallyn

Cataract Walk

Kings Bridge

River

West Tamar Rd

CLIFF GROUNDS RESERVE

Esk

Chairlift

Rotunda

WC

Cataract Gorge

Restaurant

South

Zig Zag Track

West Launceston

N

First Basin

WC

Chairlift

Pool

P

Alexandra Bridge

Basin Road

Duck Reach Track

The Blotched Blue-Tongue is Tasmania's largest lizard. It is often active at quite low temperatures and is widespread across much of northern and eastern Tasmania.

49

## Common Brushtail Possum
*Trichosurus vulpecula*

The Tasmanian form of this well-known species is larger and more woolly than the mainland form. It is abundant throughout most of Tasmania and is regularly seen within towns and suburbs, where it has adapted to living alongside humans. The Tasmanian form is also less arboreal than on the mainland and is frequently seen foraging on the ground.

It is not really necessary to search for this creature when visiting campgrounds within national parks as the Common Brushtail tends to visit these and picnic areas to scavenge for scraps. The bulk of the Common Brushtail's diet is made up of leaves of a variety of trees and shrubs, some of which are highly toxic to other animals.

## Access
There are a number of ways to reach Cataract Gorge, but here are the most direct. By foot, enjoy a ten-minute walk from the city centre to the historic Kings Bridge (near the Penny Royal complex). Walk across the bridge, then onto the Cataract Walkway. You could also catch a bus from the city, but walking is probably quicker than waiting for a bus.

If travelling by car, parking is easiest in Basin Road, West Launceston.

Another way to access Cataract Gorge by car is via the Cliff Grounds Reserve from Gorge Road in Trevallyn. This approach is through a large area of open forest with a grassy understorey.

## Facilities
Toilets, visitor displays, several kilometres of walking tracks, picnic areas, kiosk and restaurant, chairlift, swimming pool and changing rooms.

## Wildlife
The Cataract Walk from Kings Bridge into the First Basin area provides good viewpoints over the South Esk River for seeing White-faced Heron, Great Cormorant, Chestnut Teal and Silver Gull. Looking down into the bush thickets below the walkway, species such as Grey Fantail and Satin Flycatcher can be

observed, while from the forests on the steep sides across the river, depending on the season, come the calls of the Black-faced Cuckoo-Shrike, Fan-tailed Cuckoo, Golden Whistler and Laughing Kookaburra.

Arriving at the Rotunda, the track branches out to several options. While gardens and introduced trees dominate this area, big eucalypts, wattles and large numbers of tree ferns have been landscaped into the area. Introduced birds such as Peacock and Blackbird are obvious, but there are also a surprising number of native birds, especially if you meander into some of the little side tracks and gardens. In these quieter corners you can find Bassian Thrush and Brown Thornbill.

In spring and summer Scarlet and Flame Robins are often seen feeding on the lawns. The lawns near the restaurant are popular sites for Bennett's Wallaby, Tasmanian Pademelon, Southern Brown Bandicoot and Brushtail Possum. An evening wander is recommended.

The nearby Eagle Eyrie Lookout probably won't give you views of actual eagles, but both Brown Goshawk and Peregrine Falcon have been regularly recorded at Cataract Gorge.

The main walk through native bush travels above the river from the Alexandra Bridge to the historic Duck Reach power station. This walk is 2 km each way, and bird species you can expect to see include Tasmanian Native-Hen, Green Rosella, Swift Parrot (spring and early summer only), Grey Fantail, Superb Fairy-Wren,

## Yellow-throated Honeyeater
*Lichenostomus flavicollis*

This common, attractive honeyeater is an adaptable bird found in a wide range of habitats from alpine woodland to dry and wet sclerophyll forests, coastal heathland, and even parks and gardens with plenty of native shrubs. The Yellow-throated Honeyeater feeds mainly on insects such as flies, wasps, beetles and caterpillars, as well as spiders and some nectar.

This territorial and sedentary bird is vocal year-round and advertises its presence with a loud familiar 'tok-tok-tok' call.

## Spotted Pardalote
*Pardalotus punctatus*

The jewel-like Spotted Pardalote is the smallest of all pardalotes and a common resident across most of Tasmania except the extreme south-west. Commonly called a Diamond Bird, the Spotted Pardalote usually nests in burrows excavated in low banks, in the ground or even heaps of sand. During breeding, Spotted Pardalotes are usually quite visible, often ignoring a human close by as they fly to and from the nest burrow.

Outside breeding season, these little gems gather into loose groups and roam the forests, foraging for manna, lerps or other insects often high in the foliage.

Brown Thornbill, Pallid and Shining Bronze-Cuckoos (spring and summer), Striated and Spotted Pardalotes, Grey Shrike-Thrush, and Yellow-throated and Black-headed Honeyeaters. The belching sounds of the Yellow Wattlebird are never far away. A keen pair of eyes might spot a camouflaged Tawny Frogmouth at roost in the daytime; the Australian Owlet-Nightjar has also been recorded at Cataract Gorge.

This is dry, open forest in which an Echidna can often be seen digging close to the track and lizards such as the Tasmanian Tree Skink, Blotched Blue-Tongue and Metallic Skink may be seen basking in the sun.

You can return from Duck Reach by the same track, or by taking several flights of steps leading uphill behind the power station and then following an alternate track, through open casuarina forest, to return to Cataract Gorge. While easy to follow, this track is a little rougher than the direct track from the Alexandra Bridge.

When leaving the Gorge grounds, if you're on foot you could take the Zig Zag Track as an alternative to the Cataract Walk, which will give you even more opportunities for seeing birds in the dry forests. Snakes and lizards can sometimes be seen sunning themselves on this path in summer.

# 6 Tamar Island Wetlands

Just 10 minutes from the city of Launceston you can enjoy the Tamar River and its rich tidal wetlands. The Tamar Island Wetlands Reserve protects approximately 60 hectares of lagoons, mudflats and islands. Wetlands such as this are vitally important habitats for a huge diversity of animal and plant life, and being a tidal estuary with a three-metre tide makes for a regular change of bird activity.

Tamar Island is connected to the western bank of the Tamar River by a 1.5 km boardwalk. Even if you don't walk out to the island itself, good bird sightings can often be had from the shelter of the Tamar Island Wetlands Centre, which has large glass windows and wooden decks designed to give great views of the wetlands and associated bird life. The wetlands centre is located just 200 metres from the car park and is staffed by a group of wildlife-loving volunteers who are keen to share their local knowledge with visitors.

The female Superb Fairy-Wren is a brown bird with an orange-brown eye patch. The female builds a domed nest by herself during late winter or spring.

## KEY SPECIES

- Black Swan
- White-faced Heron
- Great Egret
- Purple Swamphen
- Little Grassbird
- Green and Gold Frog
- Tasmanian Tree Skink
- Freshwater Eel

## Access

The easiest way to get there is by car using the West Tamar Highway (A7). Signs between the Launceston suburbs of Riverside and Legana indicate the Tamar Island Wetlands Centre.

Another popular way of reaching the site is by cycling. While bicycles are not permitted on the boardwalk, they can be secured at the roadside car park.

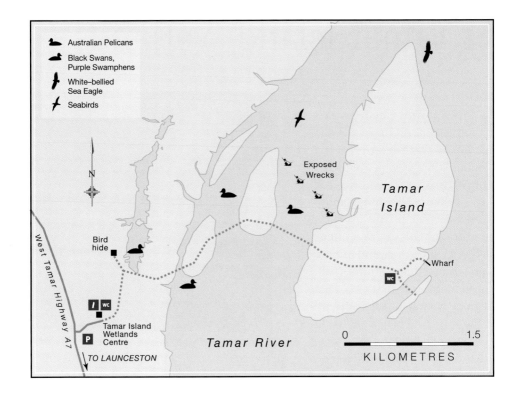

Legend:
- Australian Pelicans
- Black Swans, Purple Swamphens
- White–bellied Sea Eagle
- Seabirds

Exposed Wrecks

*Tamar Island*

Bird hide

Wharf

West Tamar Highway A7

Tamar Island Wetlands Centre

TO LAUNCESTON

*Tamar River*

0    1.5
KILOMETRES

## Dusky Moorhen
*Gallinula tenebrosa*

Although common on the Australian mainland, this medium-sized waterhen is uncommon in Tasmania, although slowly extending its range. It prefers swamps, lagoons and farm dams with plenty of aquatic and emergent vegetation and grassy banks for grazing.

The Dusky Moorhen can fly well, although is usually seen swimming. Probably the easiest place to see a Dusky Moorhen in Tasmania is on large dams in the D'Entrecasteaux Channel area of south-east Tasmania.

There is no public transport direct to the site, but a Metro bus (phone 132 201) can be taken as far as Cormiston Road, Riverside; there is then a 1.4 km walking track to the site.

There is also a floating pontoon for boat access to the island.

## Facilities

The boardwalk is open daily (except Christmas Day) from dawn until sunset. Opening times for the wetlands centre vary with the season: 10.00 a.m. to 4.00 p.m. from April through September, and 9.00 a.m. to 5.00 p.m. from October through March. Entry is via a donation.

The boarded walkway to the island is level and will suit some wheelchair users and those with prams and strollers. Tracks on the island have natural surfaces and are generally not suited to wheelchairs.

Close to the car park you'll find wheelchair-accessible toilets, a waterbird viewing area and the wetlands centre.

Tamar Island has a picnic area with gas barbecue, toilets and walking tracks.

## Wildlife

Wildlife in the wetlands is intricately connected to water, and what you see varies with the tides and water levels. Black Swans are regularly seen close to the wetlands centre—you can sometimes get quite close to adult swans with their downy, white cygnets. Even the toilet cubicles are wildlife viewpoints, with views from their windows of Little

## Swamp Rat
*Rattus lutreolus*

This small, plump rat is probably the most widespread and abundant native mammal in Tasmania, but is rarely seen in the wild due to its cryptic habits. The Swamp Rat forms tunnels through thick sedges, grasses or heath, and occurs in most habitats including forests, heathland, scrub and sedgelands, wherever there is dense ground cover.

It was originally hunted by Tasmanian Aborigines and is largely vegetarian, feeding on sedges and grasses with some fruit, seeds and insects.

## White-faced Heron
*Egretta novaehollandiae*

Tasmania's commonest heron is frequently seen in a wide range of habitats including estuaries, shallow lagoons, farm dams, paddocks and even gardens, where they forage for small fish, crustaceans, insects or worms. The nest is a loose platform of sticks built in a bush, or in a tree at up to 20 metres in height. Both male and female incubate the eggs and changeover occurs with much bill-snapping and croaking.

The White-faced Heron may be seen almost anywhere in lowland Tasmania.

Grassbirds and Superb Fairy-Wrens flitting in and out of the rushes.

The tall rush *Phragmites australis* growing beside the boardwalk is a native grass that grows to about three metres in height. This is one of the last native grasslands along the 70 km Tamar estuary, as much of the river's foreshore is now dominated by the introduced rice grass.

The boardwalk out to Tamar Island initially passes over thickets of *Phragmites*. There is a small bird hide with a seat about 500 metres from the wetlands centre, and species such as the White-faced Heron, Purple Swamphen, Dusky Moorhen and Pacific Black Duck can be observed on the lagoon.

The boardwalk crosses two small islands on its way to Tamar Island and there are two long bridges for the main water crossings. These bridges are regular roosting sites for species such as Australian Pelican, Great and Little Pied Cormorant, Crested Tern, Pacific Gull and Silver Gull. Other birds to be seen could include Great and Cattle Egrets, Swamp Harrier, Brown Falcon, Whistling Kite, White-bellied Sea-Eagle, Curlew Sand-piper, Greenshank and Red-necked Stint.

You will notice an old hide just below the boardwalk: this is from a bygone era when waterfowl hunting was permitted here. While they are still shot elsewhere, waterfowl on this section of river are now protected.

Other interesting pieces of infra-structure—and good perches for birds— are the old shipwrecks that were scuttled to the west of the island between 1926 and

1971. The aim was to divert water to the main channel east of the island to help prevent it silting up.

Once farmland, pasture grasses on the island now provide foraging ground for species such as the Tasmanian Native-Hen and Black Swan. Some small pockets of paperbark swamps provide habitat for small mammals such as the Swamp Rat and Tasmanian Pademelon. You can hear several species of frog; many will recognise the Eastern Banjo Frog. Not so well known is the Green and Gold Frog, the largest frog in Tasmania. The Tamar wetlands are a refuge for this vulnerable and declining species. They also provide the perfect home for the snake-like Freshwater Eels, which originate from spawn thousands of kilometres north in the warmer Coral Sea.

Perhaps unusually for a wetland, bordering patches of scrub and woodland provide habitat for the Tasmanian Tree Skink. This widespread lizard is endemic to Tasmania, where it is usually found in trees, often at great heights.

While you need as little as an hour to walk to the island and back, a slow and observant trip will reward with wildlife sightings. There are not too many places where you can walk so easily into the heart of a wetland. ■

## Purple Swamphen
*Porphyrio porphyrio*

Large and brightly coloured, this waterbird clambers through swamp vegetation by clasping reed stems with its large feet. It can frequently be seen grazing in wet pastures on the edges of swamps and marshes.

The nest is a trampled-down platform of reeds and is built by a group of females. Several females lay eggs in the nest; the eggs are incubated by all females, although mainly the dominant one. A nursery nest is also built for the chicks, which are mainly brooded at night.

Purple Swamphens are common in Tasmania and may be seen at Moulting Lagoon, Huon River Valley, Derwent River at Granton, Goulds Lagoon, and alongside the Tamar River.

# 7 Waterhouse Conservation Area

On the north-east coast of Tasmania, between Bridport and Tomahawk, is a glorious natural area of coastal heathland, lagoons and high sand dunes. Covering nearly 7000 hectares, the Waterhouse Conservation Area contains three large deep-water lagoons—Big Waterhouse Lake, Little Waterhouse Lake and Blackmans Lagoon—as well as many smaller well-vegetated lagoons.

The Banded Lapwing is an uncommon bird in Tasmania, where it is restricted to open grassy plains. This bird was found nesting on the airstrip on Hunter Island, to the north-west of the main island of Tasmania.

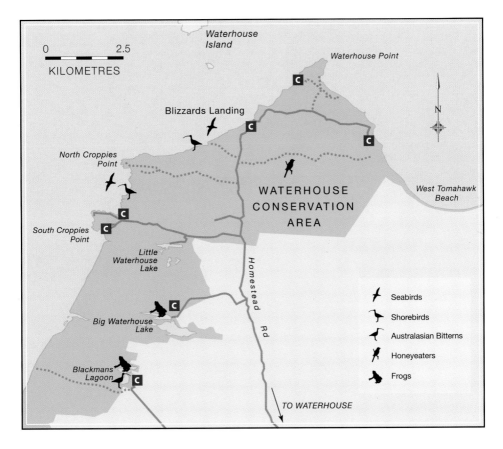

Waterhouse Island

Waterhouse Point

0    2.5
KILOMETRES

Blizzards Landing

North Croppies Point

WATERHOUSE
CONSERVATION
AREA

West Tomahawk Beach

South Croppies Point

Little Waterhouse Lake

Homestead Rd

Big Waterhouse Lake

Blackmans Lagoon

TO WATERHOUSE

N

🐟 Seabirds

🐦 Shorebirds

🐦 Australasian Bitterns

🐦 Honeyeaters

🐸 Frogs

## Access

The most direct route to the reserve is from the town of Bridport. Continue east along the B82 for approximately 27 km until you reach Waterhouse. Turn left onto Homestead Road, which leads to the Waterhouse Conservation Area.

## Facilities

There are several approved bush camping areas, but you will need to bring all your supplies with you, including drinking water. There are basic pit toilets.

## Wildlife

The main focus of this reserve is the bird life and approximately 136 species have been recorded. The sandy beaches are frequented by Pied and Sooty Oystercatchers, and Pacific and Silver Gulls. Look out for Fairy and Little Terns as they sometimes breed on this stretch of coast. Caspian and Crested Terns are also commonly seen patrolling offshore or roosting on a beach.

The lagoons are excellent for Black Swan, Hoary-headed Grebe, several duck species, Tasmanian Native-Hen

## Little Tern
*Sterna albifrons*

Tasmania's smallest tern is mainly found on east coast beaches, where it sometimes breeds in small numbers. Wholly protected in Tasmania, the Little Tern is an endangered species, with a breeding population limited to perhaps ten pairs each year.

Little Terns in Tasmania traditionally nest on sandy beaches or sand spits during late spring. Terns attempting to breed in these areas frequently suffer considerable disturbance from humans and dogs, which often results in nests, eggs or chicks being destroyed.

Fortunately, recent management in the form of temporary fencing of Little Tern nests combined with signing and wardening has helped the plight of these beautiful seabirds.

The Little Tern may be sighted at the Waterhouse Conservation Area, Mt William National Park, St Helens or Scamander area (south of St Helens Point Conservation Area).

## Spotted-tailed Quoll

*Dasyurus maculatus*

The largest Australian quoll remains common in many areas of Tasmania, but is rarely seen due to its nocturnal habits. The Spotted-tailed Quoll has thick golden-brown fur with a scattering of white spots. The long tail also has white spots of varying sizes. This beautiful creature is usually seen pacing slowly around the forest floor, although it is also an agile climber.

Spotted-tailed Quolls sometimes visit picnic areas or campgrounds for scraps and are most likely to be seen at Mt William, Cradle Mountain–Lake St Clair or Mt Field National Parks.

## Black-fronted Dotterel

*Elseyornis melanops*

This small, dapper wader prefers inland lagoons, farm dams and shingle banks of streams, where it feeds on aquatic and terrestrial insects and seeds collected from the ground. Although a wader, the Black-fronted Dotterel rarely enters the water.

A master of camouflage, this small bird is easy to miss. If disturbed, particularly when breeding, it sneaks some distance away before taking flight—or it may feign injury to lure an intruder away from its eggs or chicks.

The Black-fronted Dotterel may be seen at Moulting Lagoon and Rostrevor Lagoon (about 1 km north of Triabunna on the east coast).

## Swamp Harrier

*Circus approximans*

Sometimes referred to as 'wonky wings', Swamp Harriers are widespread and quite common in Tasmania. They are, however, unfortunately decreasing in some areas, mainly due to drainage of marshlands for agriculture.

Swamp Harriers nest on the ground in long rushes or among reeds near lagoons or marshy areas, or sometimes in fields of grain. Following breeding, birds from Tasmania migrate north across Bass Strait to over-winter on the Australian mainland.

The Swamp Harrier may be seen at Bridgewater (north-west of Hobart), South Arm, Bruny Island Neck Game Reserve, Moulting Lagoon and Narawntapu National Park.

and Black-fronted Dotterel. This is also one of the prime sites in Tasmania for seeing an Australasian Bittern. Try scanning the areas of dense reeds and other emergent vegetation for this uncommon Tasmanian bird.

The large swathes of coastal heathland are a stronghold for the Tawny-crowned and other honeyeaters.

Farmland in the area is also worth observing for birdlife such as the Australian Shelduck, White-faced Heron, Cattle Egret, Masked and Banded Lapwings, Richard's Pipit, Swamp Harrier, Brown Falcon and possibly Wedge-tailed Eagle.

Many species of marsupial occur within the reserve including the Tasmanian Devil, and Spotted-tailed and Eastern Quolls. All three of these carnivores can sometimes be seen scavenging around campsites. Other mammals include Bennett's Wallaby, Tasmanian Pademelon, Tasmanian Bettong, and possibly Eastern and Little Pygmy-Possums. The coastal heathland should provide ideal habitat for the New Holland Mouse, although it has only been recorded outside the reserve.

The lagoons and swamps also provide excellent habitat for frog species. This is probably Tasmania's major site for the Green and Gold Frog, and that voracious hunter, the Striped Marsh Frog, can also be found. ■

# 8 Flinders Island

Flinders Island is the largest of more than 50 islands that make up the Furneaux Islands in Bass Strait and are endowed with easily seen wildlife. They also have a bloody history of wildlife slaughter. The second British settlement in Australia was a sealing station established on Cape Barren Island in 1798; in less than ten years, seals in Bass Strait had been hunted almost to extinction. Today their outlook is much brighter with seals fully protected by law, populations slowly recovering, and significant areas of land reserved to protect wildlife. There are many sites to see wildlife here, including Strzelecki National Park, East Coast Lagoons and Settlement Point.

## KEY SPECIES

- Echidna
- Bennett's Wallaby
- Tasmanian Pademelon
- New Holland Mouse
- Cape Barren Goose
- Musk Duck
- Eastern Curlew
- Paper Nautilus

The tiny New Holland Mouse is a rare animal in Tasmania, being restricted to coastal heathlands of the north-east, where it prefers recently burnt areas.

# Access

Flinders Island is about 150 km north-east of Launceston. Regular air services operate from both Launceston and Melbourne, and there are also options for charter flights. If you're lucky enough to have your own boat or plane, you can take yourself to this Bass Strait wonderland.

There is no public transport on Flinders Island but options for getting around include hiring a car, bus or bicycle. You can take your own bicycle to the island, but discuss this with the airline company when booking your flight. Bicycles can also be freighted by sea.

You can also walk long distances on the island: I've known one keen birdwatcher who walked the island's entire coastline. However, this option will take you into some remote country so careful research is required.

For further information about transport,

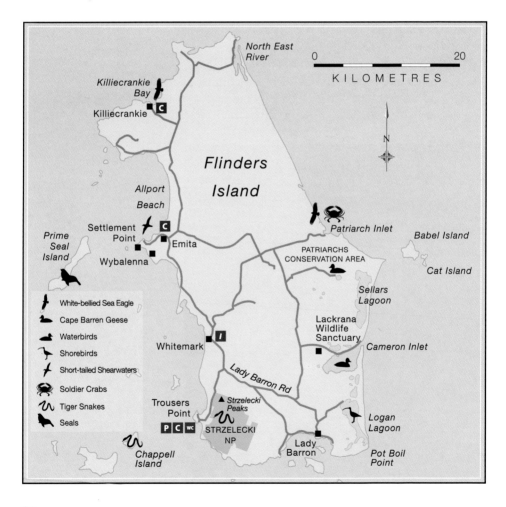

accommodation and other services, contact the Flinders Island Tourist Information Centre (phone 1800 994 477) or the Tasmanian Visitor Information Network.

## Facilities

There are several privately operated tourism services on Flinders Island, including guided wildlife tours. Most services are available in the main town of Whitemark, although supplies and accommodation can also be obtained in the town of Lady Barron.

### Strzelecki National Park

Trousers Point has toilets, a picnic area with gas barbecues, tank water, bush camping and a walking track. At Strzelecki Peaks there is a walking track to the summit.

### East Coast Lagoons

There are no facilities here so wildlife watchers should travel with food and water supplies and a good road map. There are no walking tracks and gum boots are recommended in winter, spring and early summer.

### Settlement Point

Viewing platform at the Shearwater colony.

## Wildlife

Wildlife is abundant all over Flinders Island, and over 160 bird species have been recorded here. Even a short stroll around the towns will get you close to

One of our most common macropods, the Tasmanian Pademelon is found from sea level to high alpine country. Pademelons eat grasses, herbs and some small shrubs.

birds such as the Green Rosella, New Holland Honeyeater, Grey Fantail and Beautiful Firetail. You will notice Cape Barren Geese very soon after arriving on the island. Unfortunately, you will also see many road-kill wallabies and possums, which is why slow driving at night is recommended. Wombats are particularly common in many areas, and hitting one of these harmless creatures results not only in the death of the wombat but also in possible serious damage to the vehicle.

## Australian Hobby

*Falco longipennis*

This small, dapper falcon is a fierce and dashing hunter, mainly of small birds. It frequently hunts at dusk, when it snatches large insects such as dragonflies and grasshoppers as well as bats on the wing. Hobbies lay their eggs in the old nests of corvids high in trees and line them with leaves or bark strips.

The Australian Hobby is uncommon in Tasmania but may be seen at Narawntapu National Park, in the Tasmanian Midlands or on Flinders Island.

**Strzelecki National Park**

There are two parts to this national park, which protects an area of over 4200 hectares. The larger area contains Flinders and Strzelecki Peaks, while the smaller area contains the Trousers Point area.

The larger area has the most wildlife habitat in the park, but access is limited to the steep walking track to the Strzelecki Peaks. Nonetheless, there's plenty of habitat for observing small birds such as the Pink Robin, Tasmanian Thornbill, Olive Whistler and Crescent and Yellow-throated Honeyeaters on a walk up the mountain. Close to the summit, you might see a Wedge-tailed Eagle soaring high. This very energetic walk won't suit everyone and will require some three to four hours for a return trip. Keep a look-out for Tiger Snakes, which can occur anywhere on the peaks.

The Trousers Point area is small, but among the Casuarina trees in the picnic and camping sites you might see Tasmanian Pademelon, Bennett's Wallaby or an Echidna. At night Brushtail Possum and Ringtail Possum can also be spotted. To enjoy the wildlife, camping here is recommended for those equipped for bush camping.

A one and a half hour circuit walk leads from Trousers Point to Fotheringate Beach, returning via the same route or along the road. The walk includes beaches, unusual rock features and light bush, meaning a variety of wildlife habitat.

## East Coast Lagoons

Cast your eyes over a map of Flinders Island and you will see a network of wetlands along the east coast. The large wetlands of Logan Lagoon, Cameron Inlet and Sellars Lagoon are all important migratory bird habitats, and Logan Lagoon is listed under the Convention on Wetlands of International Importance (the Ramsar Convention).

Logan Lagoon extends to over 1000 hectares and can be reached from Lady Barron by taking either the Pot Boil or Logan Lagoon roads. From the end of the Pot Boil Road, you can walk out to Pot Boil Point. Thirteen migratory birds have been recorded at Logan Lagoon and, with the exception of the Double-banded Plover, all breed in the Arctic. These summer migrants include the Red-necked Stint, Common Greenshank and Eastern Curlew.

Eight species of duck have been recorded on the island, and all occur on the east coast lagoons. These include the Musk Duck and Blue-billed Duck. My first view of a Musk Duck was on nearby Sellars Lagoon: I was certainly astonished by this strange bird with its raised tail and puffed-up under-bill lobe.

Cameron Inlet is accessed from Lackrana Road and Cameron Inlet Road. The Lackrana Wildlife Sanctuary has been sown with pasture to provide habitat for Cape Barren Geese. Cameron Inlet can contain any of the migratory species mentioned for Logan Lagoon, and the area between these two water bodies is an important feeding area for wetland birds.

## Pacific Gull

*Larus pacificus*

Mainly restricted to the coasts, the Pacific Gull is an impressive bird with the largest bill of any gull. A rather solitary bird, it prefers offshore islands, headlands and beaches, although in Tasmania it frequently visits rubbish tips to scavenge. It feeds on a variety of fish, squid, crabs, sea urchins and molluscs, which are collected from beaches, rocks or from the sea. Hard-shelled prey are dropped from a height onto rocks to break open; the same rocks are often used for many years and develop into shell 'middens'.

Pacific Gulls nest singly or in small scattered colonies on many of Tasmania's offshore islands.

67

## Bennett's Wallaby

*Macropus rufogriseus*

This large wallaby is widespread across much of Tasmania and is frequently referred to incorrectly as a kangaroo. Largely a grazing animal, Bennett's Wallaby is found throughout a variety of habitats wherever suitable cover exists. It is also common in alpine areas and is easily seen at many of the sites in this book.

It is also common on the south-east mainland, where it is known as the Red-necked Wallaby.

As Logan Lagoon is often dry in summer, Cameron Inlet is important summer habitat. A huge number of wetland birds use this inlet including cormorants, grebes, ducks, egrets, herons and pelicans.

Sellars Lagoon is accessed from Summers Road and there are numerous small lagoons within walking distance of the privately owned Patriarchs Conservation Area. From here an easy walk leads to the top of South Patriarch where you will have terrific views of Babel Island, which has a Short-tailed Shearwater colony of three million birds.

Flinders, together with many of the other offshore islands, holds an important population of White-bellied Sea-Eagles; several pairs breed here each year. These spectacular birds of prey can be seen almost anywhere in coastal areas, but prime sites include Killiecrankie Bay, Patriarch Inlet and Cameron Inlet.

Flinders is excellent for other raptors including the Wedge-tailed Eagle, Brown Goshawk, Collared Sparrowhawk, Australian Hobby, Peregrine Falcon, Nankeen Kestrel and Swamp Harrier.

Just south-east of Babel Island lies Cat Island, which was the site of possibly the largest Australasian Gannet colony within Australian waters, numbering approximately 10,000 birds in 1908. Unfortunately this vibrant gannet colony was systematically destroyed, largely by fishermen taking the gannets as crayfish bait. Although no gannets currently breed on this island, attempts have been made during the last 20 years to attract gannets to recolonise using decoy birds.

Surrounding the main islands of Flinders, Cape Barren and Clarke are myriad small islands that hold important colonies of a variety of seabirds. Difficulty of access thankfully offers added protection to the wildlife on these islands, and many are nature reserves requiring a permit to land. Breeding seabirds on these islands include the Little Penguin, Short-tailed Shearwater, White-faced Storm Petrel, Common Diving-Petrel, Australian Pelican, Black-faced Cormorant, Pacific and Silver Gulls, the Caspian, Crested and White-fronted Terns, and Pied and Sooty Oystercatchers. The White-fronted Tern is a rare breeding bird in Tasmania which only nests on a few small islands in Bass Strait.

The Cape Barren Goose came perilously close to extinction from indiscriminate shooting but has now recovered due to protection. Around 4000 pairs now breed in the Furneaux Islands, and these numbers are still increasing.

Fourteen mammal species occur on Flinders Island and all can be found in the area of the East Coast Lagoons. These species include the New Holland Mouse, which is listed as rare under the Tasmanian *Threatened Species Act*.

## Cape Barren Goose
*Cereopsis novaehollandiae*

Endemic to Australia, these distinctive waterfowl spend most of their time on land. Although not typical geese, they do graze like geese and are strong fliers. Cape Barren Geese probably mate for life, and they breed during winter. Nests are usually built on the ground, although at times they may be sited several metres above ground in bushes or Tea-Tree scrub.

They prefer the coasts and islands of southern Australia, with the Bass Strait islands being a stronghold. The easiest place to see them in the wild is Maria Island, where they have been introduced.

## Musk Duck
*Biziura lobata*

This rather strange-looking diving duck prefers deep and usually permanent freshwater lakes and swamps. Musk Ducks dive quietly, are able to swim under water and can remain submerged for over a minute.

The courtship display of the male is most extraordinary. First he throws jets of water behind him with a series of powerful kicks. Then, raising his head, he inflates his cheeks and neck and expands the bladder that hangs under his bill. At the same time he raises the tail fan-like over his body, and as he sinks back into the water he utters a piercing whistle.

Musk Ducks may be seen at the east coast lagoons on Flinders Island, Narawntapu National Park and in the vicinity of Bridgewater, north-west of Hobart.

### Settlement Point

Access is from the township of Emita through the Wybalenna site that is owned by the Tasmanian Aboriginal community. Settlement Point has a large Short-tailed Shearwater colony and the birds can be seen from late September until early May (except for a few weeks in November). A viewing platform is located right in the colony. Wear windproof clothing, take something comfortable to sit on, wait until dark and you'll have birds swooping low over your head as they return to their burrows.

### Other places of interest

The Castle Rock walk from near Allport Beach as well as Killiecrankie Bay are recommended. Look for the spiralled shells of the Paper Nautilus (a type of octopus) that Flinders Island beaches are famed for.

The many offshore islands offer history, spectacular scenery and opportunities to view wildlife such as Australian Fur Seals. Enquire at the Tourist Information Centre in Whitemark for touring options.

Many of the smaller islands in the Furneaux group are now owned by the Tasmanian Aboriginal community. Anybody wishing to visit any of these islands should first check on ownership and then request permission from the Aboriginal Land Council of Tasmania or one of the private leaseholders. ■

# 9 Mt William National Park

Mt William National Park in the far north-east corner is another of Tasmania's glorious coastal parks. Extending to almost 14,000 hectares, this enticing area has the state's mildest climate, and long, deserted, dazzling white beaches formed from the high content of quartz in the local granite. Scarcely populated, it contains a wealth of interesting wildlife and comprises huge swathes of magnificent coastal heathland, dry sclerophyll woodland and open grassy plains, bordered to the north and south by two coastal lagoons at Musselroe Bay and Ansons Bay.

## KEY SPECIES

- Echidna
- Tasmanian Devil
- Spotted-tailed Quoll
- Common Wombat
- Forester Kangaroo
- New Holland Mouse
- Wedge-tailed Eagle
- Hooded Plover

The female Common Wombat has a backward-facing pouch. This female wombat's pouch is dragging on the ground due to the large joey inside.

71

## Access

Two main roads lead to Mt William National Park. The first road (C845) from Gladstone to Musselroe Bay leads to the northern section of the park. At the entrance to the right of the road is a park staff-house.

The second option is to drive north from St Helens to Ansons Bay (C843) and follow the road to Eddystone Point at the southern end of the park.

## Facilities

Accommodation is limited to four camping areas with basic toilets, fireplaces and picnic tables in the northern area. Electric barbecues are available at campground No. 4 at Stumpys Bay in the north of the park. Campsites are also available at the southern end of the park, at the end of the beachside road between Deep Creek and Eddystone Point.

The circular Forester Kangaroo Drive leads to the right from Musselroe Road and leads back to the C845. Northern camp areas and a road to Mt William peak may be accessed from here.

No power is available at any camping area, and there is no fresh drinking water in Mt William National Park.

At Gladstone there is a hotel and general store, with fuel also available.

## Wildlife

Mt William National Park was originally proclaimed to protect the state's last remaining population of Forester Kangaroos—all of Tasmania's other

Echidnas (opposite) have extremely powerful feet and claws that allow them to dig rapidly into soil to escape danger or to dig for ants.

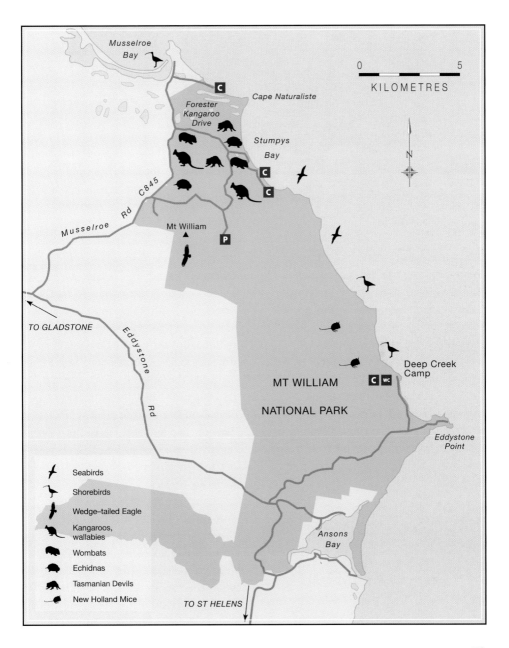

## Silver Gull
*Larus novaehollandiae*

This nomadic and adaptable seabird is common across most of Australia and Tasmania where it may be seen in towns, cities and rubbish tips, as well as coastal areas. It is one of the few birds to have benefited from European settlement, particularly by people feeding them scraps on beaches or in parks.

Silver Gulls are able to scavenge on a wide variety of foods, such as crustaceans, plankton and invertebrates in coastal habitats, or worms, insects and their larvae in agricultural paddocks or city parks.

populations were exterminated by early settlers in the nineteenth century. Forester Kangaroos remain common here and are easily seen from Forester Kangaroo Drive. Bennett's Wallaby, Tasmanian Pademelon and Common Wombat also occur in large numbers throughout the park. Brush-tailed Possums remain common and are frequently encountered near the campgrounds.

The Mt William area is also one of the easier sites in Tasmania to watch Echidnas foraging. The Tasmanian Echidna is visibly furrier than its mainland counterpart, with fewer spines.

Mt William National Park has traditionally been one of Tasmania's best sites to see Australia's two largest dasyurids, the Spotted-tailed Quoll and the Tasmanian Devil. Unfortunately, Tasmanian Devils are at present far less common than formerly, due to Devil Facial Tumour Disease. Being largely scavengers, they regularly patrol the beaches and their tracks are frequently found in the sand.

Although the Spotted-tailed Quoll is more usually found in the forests of western and southern Tasmania, this unique nocturnal carnivore does have a healthy population in the Mt William area. Rarely seen during daylight hours, they are frequent visitors to its camping areas, where they scavenge for scraps.

# Wedge-tailed Eagle
*Aquila audax*

This magnificent bird is Tasmania's largest bird of prey, with a wingspan of up to 2.5 metres. Unfortunately this endemic sub-species is classified as endangered, with a declining population of approximately 75 breeding pairs. In Tasmania it nests only in old-growth native forests. Many of these forests are on private land and are threatened with clearing for forestry or agriculture.

Wedge-tailed Eagles may be seen at many of the sites in this book including Mt William, Maria Island and Freycinet National Parks, as well as Mt Wellington and Tinderbox Peninsula on Hobart's doorstep.

As always, visitors should refrain from feeding any wildlife. Wallabies and other Tasmanian marsupials may develop a debilitating disease called 'lumpy jaw' when fed processed food. The large areas of coastal heathland provide the perfect habitat for the rare New Holland Mouse, which reaches its highest densities at Mt William. Coastal heathland here is subject to a regime of managed burning, providing a mosaic of differing age structures within the vegetation to ensure the optimal habitat requirements for the New Holland Mouse.

## Red-capped Plover
*Charadrius ruficapillus*

Due to its wide tolerance of a range of habitats, this small plover remains common in Tasmania and is found along sandy beaches, dunes and even on the shores of inland lakes, lagoons and farm dams.

The nest is usually placed in a slack between dunes, on a sandy rise above a beach, or even on a grassy verge or exposed ridge bordering a lake or lagoon. The nest itself is a small scrape, usually lined with pieces of shell or scraps of plant material. It may contain two or three eggs, which are extremely well camouflaged as they are sandy-coloured with dark markings.

A wide range of bird species is found, with approximately 100 species recorded. Being coastal, a wide range of seabirds may be seen, including the Australasian Gannet, Short-tailed Shearwater, Caspian and Crested Terns, and Kelp, Pacific and Silver Gulls. Pied and Sooty Oyster-catchers are common on the beaches, and the declining Hooded and Red-capped Plovers also breed on the beaches.

The low-growing coastal heathland is home to a wealth of birds including the Crescent, New Holland, Yellow-throated and Tawny-crowned Honeyeaters, Scarlet, Dusky and Flame Robins, Beautiful Firetail and Yellow Wattlebird. Tasmanian Native-Hens are common, and flocks of raucous Yellow-tailed Black Cockatoos are often seen feeding in the banksia bushes.

Wedge-tailed Eagles breed within the park and White-bellied Sea-Eagles can sometimes be seen patrolling the coast.

Approximately 8 km north of Eddystone Point is a group of small islands known as Georges Rocks, which are included in Mt William National Park. These small islands are extremely attractive to a variety of seabirds, and several species breed, including the Little Penguin, White-faced Storm Petrel, Short-tailed Shearwater, Common Diving Petrel, Black-faced Cormorant, Hooded Plover, Sooty Oystercatcher, Pacific and Silver Gulls, and Caspian and Crested Terns.

It is important that people refrain from landing on these islands during spring and summer to restrict disturbance to the breeding seabirds.

Musselroe Bay, just to the north of the national park, is an excellent site for viewing seabirds and waterfowl. This shallow lagoon is popular with Australian Pelicans, which breed on a few small islands in Bass Strait. Look for Fairy or Little Terns, which sometimes fish here.

## Sooty Oystercatcher
*Haematopus fuliginosus*

Compared with the Pied Oystercatcher, the Sooty Oystercatcher prefers rockier coastlines, headlands and exposed rocky reefs, which means it enjoys less disturbance. The two varieties otherwise share similar habits.

The nest of the Sooty Oystercatcher is often placed in a cleft in rocks, and is usually built up with a collection of small pebbles, shells or seaweed.

# 10 St Helens area

## KEY SPECIES

- Australian Pelican
- Double-banded Plover
- Hooded Plover
- Little Tern
- Fairy Tern
- Caspian Tern
- Tawny-crowned Honeyeater

St Helens is a small but popular holiday town on the east coast approximately 170 km east of Launceston along the Tasman Highway (A3). Close to the township are several coastal reserves which attract a diverse range of birds. The area has a mild climate and receives quite low rainfall.

## Access

### Bay of Fires Coastal Reserve

Take the road (C850) north-east from St Helens to Binalong Bay. Then take the road (C848) north. This road passes through the conservation area, which extends north to the Gardens.

### St Helens Point State Conservation Area

The southern section may be accessed by taking the Tasman Highway south for 6 km to Dianas Basin. To

Copperhead Snakes prefer wet, marshy areas where they prey on frogs and other small invertebrates. Although venomous they are not usually aggressive.

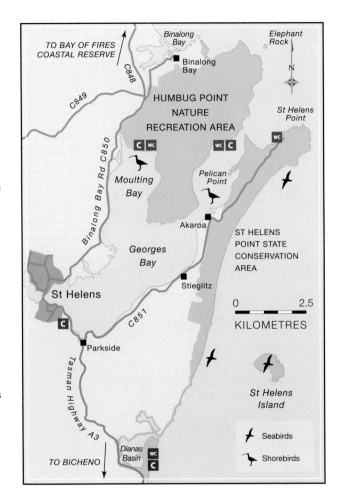

access the northern section drive south on the Tasman Highway to Parkside. Turn left at Parkside and continue for about 11 km to St Helens Point.

## Facilities

### Bay of Fires Coastal Reserve

There are several well-signed basic camping areas with pit toilets. There is no food, petrol or fresh water available north of Binalong Bay.

### St Helens Point State Conservation Area

There are only basic camp areas, plus wheelchair-accessible toilets at Dianas Basin and St Helens Point.

## Wildlife

### Bay of Fires Coastal Reserve

This attractive coastal reserve is approximately 12 km north of St Helens and protects an area of rocky headlands and long sandy beaches, plus several lagoons and areas of coastal heathland. Birds to be seen here should include the Australian Pelican, Australasian Gannet, Great, Little Pied and Black-faced Cormorants, Great and Little Egrets, Black Swan, Australian Shelduck, Pacific Black Duck, Chestnut and Grey Teals, Musk Duck, White-bellied Sea-Eagle, Brown Falcon, Pacific and Kelp Gulls, and Caspian and Crested Terns. Little and Fairy Terns sometimes breed on the beaches in

## Fairy Tern
*Sterna nereis*

Like the Little Tern, the Fairy Tern is uncommon in Tasmania, but does sometimes breed in small colonies. It is restricted to coastal areas and breeds on sandy beaches or sand spits right around the Tasmanian coast as well as on the Bass Strait islands.

The long-term survival of this delightful tern is threatened by the increasing use of beaches by people and four-wheel-drive vehicles, dogs and horses. This frequently causes desertion of nests or destruction of eggs and chicks, often inadvertently. To protect these and other beach-nesting birds we believe that prime sites for these birds should be out of bounds to humans during the breeding season.

## Grey Teal
*Anas gracilis*

A common duck, Grey Teal may be seen in any watery habitat including salt, brackish or fresh water. As with many other waterfowl they are able to breed at almost any time of the year depending on rainfall, although this does normally mean springtime in Tasmania. They employ a variety of nest sites ranging from tree hollows and rabbit holes to a simple crevice in the ground among rocks or vegetation.

Grey Teal may be seen at the lagoon at Narawntapu National Park, Moulting Lagoon and Goulds Lagoon.

this area, and Hooded and Red-capped Plovers breed regularly.

The coastal heathland supports Tawny-crowned Honeyeaters, while Yellow-tailed Black-Cockatoos may be seen feeding on banksia bushes.

On the northern shore of Georges Bay are extensive areas of tidal mudflats which attract a variety of waders such as Greenshank, Bar-tailed Godwit, Eastern Curlew, Lesser Golden Plover, Sharp-tailed Sandpiper, Red-necked Stint, Pied and Sooty Oystercatchers, Masked Lapwing and, in winter, the Double-banded Plover.

There are normally several Australian Pelicans to be seen in Georges Bay. The spectacular Australian Pelican is an uncommon bird in Tasmania, although it does breed on a couple of small islands in Bass Strait. Ruddy Turnstone is also a

## Caspian Tern
*Sterna caspia*

Terns are seabirds that are closely related to gulls, but with long, pointed wings and short legs. The impressive Caspian Tern is the largest of all terns and has a massive, dagger-like scarlet bill. It feeds on small fish, which it catches by plunge-diving from a height of ten to twenty metres, often after hovering for a few seconds.

Caspian Terns are usually seen singly or in pairs patrolling coastlines, estuaries and lagoons, but also range inland onto lakes and rivers. This spectacular seabird breeds on many of Tasmania's small offshore islands. It is threatened by competition from the increasingly populous Kelp Gull and by disturbance by humans while breeding.

## Australian Pelican
### *Pelecanus conspicillatus*

This large, well-known waterbird is uncommon in Tasmania, but does breed on a few small islets within Bass Strait. The nest is a loose platform of twigs and plants formed on the ground, and the birds are extremely skittish and liable to desert the nest if disturbed.

Pelicans are magnificent fliers and are able to soar to great heights. Fossil remains of pelicans have been found dating back 30 to 40 million years and have probably changed little since.

Australian Pelicans may be seen in small numbers at several sites in Tasmania, including St Helens, Little Swanport (south of Swansea), Great Musselroe Bay (north of Mt William National Park), Orielton Lagoon (near the town of Sorell), Narawntapu National Park, Tamar Island Wetlands, Flinders Island and on the Huon River south of Hobart.

possibility here, although these are more usually sighted north in Ansons Bay, near Mt William National Park.

This mix of dry habitats is also excellent for mammals such as Bennett's Wallaby, Tasmanian Pademelon and Common Wombat. Tasmanian Devil and Spotted-tailed Quoll frequent the area, and Brushtail Possum is common. The dry woodland provides perfect conditions for Echidnas, while a few Forester Kangaroos also inhabit the area.

### St Helens Point State Conservation Area

This coastal reserve stretches from Dianas Basin in the south to St Helens Point in the north and protects a range of habitats including coastal heathland, large areas of sand dunes and wetlands. Birds seen here are similar to those recorded for Bay of Fires, above. Basic camp sites are available at St Helens Point, Dianas Basin and Stieglitz Beach.

Small offshore islets in this area, such as St Helens Island and Paddys Island, are very attractive to breeding seabirds including Little Penguin, White-faced Storm-Petrel, Short-tailed Shearwater, Black-faced Cormorant, Pacific and Silver Gulls, Crested and Caspian Terns, and Sooty Oystercatcher. ■

# 11 Bicheno area

This charming town on Tasmania's east coast is a very popular destination in summer. Bicheno is an ideal base for exploring the nearby Douglas–Apsley National Park and has the finest Little Penguin viewing area on the east coast.

Birdlife is much in evidence in and around Bicheno and many gardens contain native shrubs and trees which are attractive to birds. Expect to see Swift Parrots during spring, when eucalypts are flowering. Other birds to be seen include Galah, Little Wattlebird and other honeyeaters and Australian Magpie. The attractive beach is a good site for Hooded and Red-capped Plovers, with terns fishing offshore.

## KEY SPECIES

- Tasmanian Devil
- Eastern Quoll
- Tasmanian Bettong
- Little Penguin
- Wedge-tailed Eagle
- Crested Tern
- Swift Parrot

**CRESTED TERN**
*Sterna bergii*

The Crested Tern is one of the most abundant and familiar of Tasmania's seabirds. It lives on the island year-round, mainly on coasts and estuaries, but also upstream on some tidal rivers. During spring, Crested Terns congregate to nest in often large colonies on ancestral offshore breeding islands. Highly nomadic, their breeding range extends throughout the Indian Ocean, South-East Asia and much of the western and central Pacific.

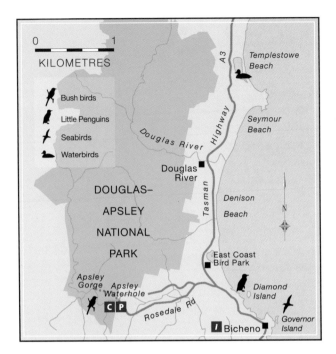

The Douglas–Apsley area was proclaimed a national park in 1989, following a concerted campaign by conservationists. This recent national park protects a large area of dry eucalypt forest, together with flower-studded heathlands, deep river gorges and plunging waterfalls.

## Access

For Bicheno, take the Tasman Highway (A3) from Hobart. Bicheno is approx-imately 175 km north-east of Hobart and 170 km south-east of Launceston.

### Governor and Diamond Islands

To access Governor Island, head for the small harbour at the southern end of town. Governor Island can then be seen offshore.

Being a reserve, access to this island is restricted. To access Diamond Island nature reserve, simply follow the beach north from the town. Diamond Island is approximately 1 km north of the town centre.

### Douglas–Apsley National Park

The park is situated two and a half hours (185 km) north-east of Hobart, just over two hours (160 km) south-east of Launceston, and about 10 km north-west of Bicheno.

The main access route is at the southern end of the park and leads to the car park and Apsley Waterhole. Take the Tasman Highway (A3) north of Bicheno. After 3 km turn left onto Rosedale Road. Follow this road for about 7.5 km to the main car park.

## Facilities

The attractive coastal town of Bicheno has a wide range of facilities, including motels, a caravan park, several guest-houses, shops, restaurants, and a youth hostel. There are no facilities on either Governor or Diamond Island.

**Douglas–Apsley National Park**

The Douglas–Apsley National Park has a car park and signposted walk to the waterhole. Ten minutes walk from the car park is a basic bush-camping area with pit toilets.

## Wildlife

### Diamond Island

Just north of Bicheno is Diamond Island, which at low tide is linked to the mainland by a sandy bank that can be waded across. A close watch must be kept on tide times so you don't become stranded on Diamond Island.

This stretch of coast is a prime viewing area for Little Penguins, which nest in burrows in the dunes, under rocks and even under the floors of outhouses or garages. The Little Penguin is superbly adapted to diving at sea, having a streamlined body and wings that have evolved into flippers, allowing the world's smallest penguin to literally 'fly' underwater.

Little Penguins spend most of their life at sea and, apart from breeding, only come ashore after dark to visit the nest or to roost. At dusk, groups of Little Penguins gather in the surf before clambering ashore to their burrows.

### Dusky Woodswallow
*Artamus cyanopterus*

These familiar summer visitors prefer wooded habitats and usually nest in small, loose colonies. During courtship, Dusky Woodswallows engage in mutual feeding when the female, with quivering, extended wings, begs for food from her mate. Both male and female help in building the nest—an untidy basket of small roots, grass and twigs. The nest is frequently built in an exposed position such as on a fork of a branch, wedged behind a piece of bark or in an open tree hollow.

Dusky Woodswallows feed mainly by hawking for insects on the wing and can frequently be seen flying in graceful circles—interspersed with fluttering—around the canopies of trees. This attractive migrant is more common in the drier north and east of the state.

## Tasmanian Bettong
*Bettongia gaimardi*

A small wallaby, the Tasmanian Bettong remains widespread in areas of suitable habitat. It prefers dry, open, grassy woodlands which are prone to fire, avoiding wetter forests and rainforests. It formerly also occupied the south-east mainland but was wiped out early in the twentieth century due to predation by foxes and feral cats.

The Tasmanian Bettong could very soon be driven to extinction if the European Fox becomes established in Tasmania.

If visiting an adult or chick at the nest, the penguins greet each other with excited yelps or hoarse braying.

Unfortunately, Little Penguins are decreasing throughout their range due to a variety of factors. In particular, many Tasmanian beaches are becoming increasingly popular with holidayers, and in previous years there were virtually no controls on building shacks or holiday homes, so Little Penguin colonies have become increasingly subject to disturbance. In the past, the birds were even used as bait by fishermen.

Uncontrolled dogs and feral cats are a particular menace to Little Penguins, especially during the breeding season when the penguins are incubating eggs or brooding chicks in their burrows. Foxes have wreaked havoc at many Little Penguin colonies on the Australian mainland and the same would happen if they were to become established in Tasmania. On top of all this, Little Penguins are frequently run over on roads at night, usually unintentionally.

To watch Little Penguins near Bicheno it is best to join a guided tour led by an experienced naturalist. Details of the tours are advertised in the Bicheno Information Centre.

### Governor Island

Less than 200 metres off the coast of Bicheno is the Governor Island Marine Nature Reserve, covering an area of 60 hectares. The reserve includes Governor Island, Alligator Rock and the surrounding waters.

Governor Island itself is well known for harbouring one of Tasmania's largest colonies of Crested Terns. Surrounding the island is a rocky reef that drops steeply into deep water. This is a popular haunt for divers, with its clear waters, spectacular underwater scenery such as caves and sheer rock walls, and diverse range of fish and other marine organisms.

### Douglas–Apsley National Park

Over 60 species of bird have been recorded in this park, including most of the Tasmanian endemics such as the Tasmanian Native-Hen, Green Rosella, Dusky Robin, Scrubtit, Black Currawong,

## Australian Magpie
*Gymnorhina tibicen*

The organ-like, jumbled carolling of the Australian Magpie is one of the most cherished sounds of the Australian bush. This popular bird takes its name from the European Magpie, to which it is not related. In fact it is related to the butcherbirds, but has evolved into a ground-feeding insectivore.

Australian Magpies require trees with open areas of grass or bare ground, including farmland, golf courses, orchards, parks and even suburban gardens. In Tasmania they are widespread across much of the drier central and eastern parts of the state, but are absent from the wetter west.

## Galah
*Cacatua rosiecapilla*

The Galah is an adaptable bird that has managed to take advantage of European settlement. This colourful cockatoo has only recently become established in Tasmania, where it is slowly increasing in numbers and expanding its range. It is possible that a few migrants managed to cross Bass Strait, but it is equally probable that some birds have escaped from aviaries or have even been released illegally.

As with most parrots, Galahs nest in tree hollows, which could result in increased competition with native Tasmanian hole-nesters due to a limited and decreasing number of hollows.

and Yellow-throated, Strong-billed and Black-headed Honeyeaters.

En route from Bicheno to the park entrance, look out for Brown Falcon and Swamp Harrier ('wonky wings'). Other interesting birds to be seen in the park could include the Wedge-tailed Eagle (breeding), Musk Lorikeet, Tawny Frogmouth, Bassian Thrush, Pink Robin, Spotted Quail-Thrush, Beautiful Firetail and Dusky Woodswallow. The Owlet Nightjar has been recorded, but being nocturnal is a very difficult bird to see.

Many species of mammal have been recorded, although most are not easily observed due to their nocturnal lifestyles. Eastern and Spotted-tailed Quolls and the Tasmanian Devil can be found here. The park's dry sclerophyll habitat also provides perfect conditions for the Tasmanian Bettong, which requires an open, grassy understorey. It is important that a certain amount of controlled burning takes place to maintain these open grassy conditions and to provide the bettongs with the fruiting underground fungi on which they feed.

The most easily seen mammals should include Bennett's Wallaby, Tasmanian Pademelon, and Brushtail and Common Ringtail Possums.

The Australian or Southern Grayling—a rare freshwater fish which was once common in Tasmanian streams but has declined rapidly—still occurs in the Douglas River and has been seen in the Apsley Gorge. ■

# 12 Moulting Lagoon

Moulting Lagoon is a vast, shallow estuary at the mouths of the Swan and Apsley Rivers on Tasmania's east coast. This superb site is situated just north-west of Freycinet National Park and a few kilometres south-west of Bicheno. The southern boundary of Moulting Lagoon is Nine Mile Beach, at the end of which is a narrow ocean outlet into Great Oyster Bay.

This is a magnificent area for wildlife, with the Hazards of Freycinet National Park providing a scenic backdrop. Moulting Lagoon Game Reserve protects an area of approximately 4750 hectares. The lagoon contains areas of both deep and shallow water and is surrounded by large periodically exposed saltmarsh and mudflats. Most of Moulting

## KEY SPECIES

- White-bellied Sea-Eagle
- Swamp Harrier
- Black Swan
- Australasian Bittern
- Great Egret
- Sharp-tailed Sandpiper

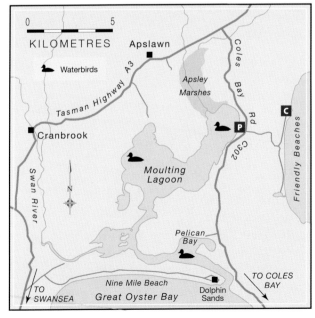

Approximately 80–100 White-bellied Sea-Eagle pairs breed in Tasmania. They build huge stick nests, mainly high in large eucalypts not far from water.

Lagoon is a Ramsar site, together with the adjacent Apsley Marshes.

## Access

From Hobart take the Tasman Highway (A3) and continue for approximately 160 km until you reach the historic township of Swansea. Moulting Lagoon is approximately 10 km north-east of Swansea.

As it covers such a vast area, there are several points of access, although most of the surrounding land is privately owned.

One option is to head north along the Tasman Highway (A3) from Swansea and take the first road on the right to Nine Mile Beach and Dolphin Sands. This gives access to the southern side of Moulting Lagoon. Alternatively, continue north along the Tasman Highway and at the bottom of the steep hill look for Sherbourne Road, which turns off to the

## Hardhead
*Aythya australis*

This fast-flying duck is a regular—if uncommon—visitor to Tasmania, where it may sometimes be seen on large lagoons or slow-flowing sections of large rivers. Related to the pochards, the Hardhead is a true diving duck and is able to feed underwater for over a minute. It is largely vegetarian, eating the seeds, flowers and vegetative parts of sedges, grasses, docks and other aquatic plants. It also feeds on some animal matter such as small fish, crustaceans and aquatic insects.

In Tasmania the nomadic Hardhead may sometimes be seen at Granton (near Bridgewater, just north-west of Hobart) and nearby Goulds Lagoon, as well as Rostrevor Lagoon (about 1 km north of Triabunna on the east coast).

## Great Egret
*Ardea alba*

The Great Egret is the largest heron in Tasmania, where it may be seen regularly each autumn or winter. This rare heron is easily recognised due to its large size and very long neck, which frequently has a kink in it. It is able to feed in quite deep water owing to its long legs, and preys primarily on small fish, amphibians, crustaceans and aquatic insects.

In Tasmania it may be spotted in the Huon River estuary, Moulting Lagoon, the Derwent River near Granton, or in other suitable habitat.

right about 1 km before the township of Apslawn.

Another option is to continue north on the A3 past Apslawn and turn right onto Coles Bay Road (C302). This road passes close to the edge of Moulting Lagoon in several places, where you will find two car parks. Alternatively, from the junction with the Tasman Highway, continue along Coles Bay Road (C302) for approximately 18 km. Look for a track to the right (Flacks Road) which leads to Pelican Bay.

## Facilities
The attractive, historic town of Swansea contains a range of shops, a motel, a caravan park and guest houses. There are very few developed facilities close to Moulting Lagoon, except for a few car parks.

## Wildlife
Moulting Lagoon is an important breeding area for Black Swans. These large and spectacular waterfowl breed in colonies or small groups in the Apsley Marshes and on some islands on the lagoon. The lagoon is also an important staging area, with high summer concentrations of Australian Shelduck, Chestnut Teal, Greenshank and Sharp-tailed Sandpiper.

Other birds to be seen here include the Australian Pelican, Black-faced, Great and Little Pied Cormorants, Great, Little and Cattle Egrets, White-faced Heron, Australasian Bittern, Pacific Black Duck, Grey Teal, Australasian Shoveler, Hardhead, Blue-billed Duck, Musk Duck, Purple Swamphen, Tasmanian Native-Hen,

Eurasian Coot, White-bellied Sea-Eagle, Wedge-tailed Eagle, Swamp Harrier, Brown Falcon, and Caspian and Crested Terns.

At the south-east corner of Moulting Lagoon is Pelican Bay, which has an extensive area of mudflats and marshes. Birds to be seen here include several wader species such as the Eastern Curlew, Greenshank, Bar-tailed Godwit, Lesser Golden Plover, Sharp-tailed Sandpiper, Curlew Sandpiper, Latham's Snipe, Red-necked Stint and Black-fronted Dotterel.

The large areas of scrub and dry woodland surrounding Moulting Lagoon are home to a wide range of passerines (perching birds) similar to those listed for the walk over the Hazards to Wineglass Bay in the adjacent Freycinet National Park. ■

## Black Swan
### Cygnus atratus

An extremely beautiful swan, particularly in flight, when the white primary feathers are visible. Black Swans fly with heavy, noisy wing-beats, frequently at night. Their musical trumpetings may be heard over a long distance, with the male call deeper than the female.

In Tasmania they normally breed during winter, with the new spring growth of grasses feeding the newly hatched cygnets. After breeding they moult and become flightless, when they may gather in large numbers on lakes and lagoons such as Moulting Lagoon on the east coast. Black Swans nest in swamps, lagoons and even farm dams right across Tasmania, with several hundred nesting in colonies or small groups at Moulting Lagoon.

# 13 Freycinet National Park

This truly magical place is one of Tasmania's most popular national parks. It extends for approximately 50 km along Tasmania's east coast and covers almost 17,000 hectares.

Freycinet Peninsula was declared a national park in 1916 and along with Mt Field it shares the distinction of being Tasmania's first national park. Later, in 1967, the spectacular Schouten Island was added, followed in 1992 by a further large area at Friendly Beaches.

The park is noted for its large variety of visible wildlife and for its spectacular granite peaks and bluffs soaring over some of Tasmania's most beautiful broad, glistening white beaches. It harbours a wide range of habitats, from dry eucalypt forests to extensive coastal dunes, patches of flower-rich heathland and shallow wetlands. This magnificent area is a veritable paradise for the wildlife enthusiast as well as walkers or climbers.

The attractively marked Mountain Dragon (opposite) is the only member of the Agamidae family to be found in Tasmania, where it prefers the dry rocky areas of the east.

## Access

From either Hobart or Launceston, Freycinet is about two and a half to three hours by road. On the Tasman Highway (A3) about 12 km south of Bicheno, take the Coles Bay Road (C302) turn-off east into the national park. The Friendly Beaches area is accessed via a gravel road leading from the Coles Bay Road about 2 km after leaving the Tasman Highway.

## Facilities

A full range of accommodation is available in and around the small township of Coles Bay, which adjoins the north-western corner of the national park. There is also a general store in Coles Bay.

Park staff are based at Freycinet National Park year-round. A visitor centre is located just inside the park entrance and is open daily from 8 a.m. to 5 p.m. The visitor centre has a park shop selling a wide range of products including park passes, camera film, postcards, clothing and natural history books.

Picnic tables, electric barbecues, toilets and water are available at Honeymoon Bay and Ranger Creek.

A campground is located at the park entrance, but as it is extremely popular during the Christmas/New Year holidays, bookings are essential and a ballot system is in operation. Basic camping is permitted at sites close to the Friendly Beaches.

## Wildlife

Tame Bennett's Wallabies and abundant Tasmanian Pademelons are easily seen at

Following protection, the endangered Humpback Whale is now seen more frequently, especially in sheltered bays on the east coast such as at Freycinet.

most picnic areas and campgrounds on the peninsula. As these mammals are nocturnal you do need to be camping overnight for close-up views. Also commonly seen are the Brushtail Possum, Eastern Quoll, Long-nosed Potoroo, Tasmanian Devil, introduced Sugar Glider and Common Ringtail Possum.

I well remember camping on Schouten Island many years ago. To my astonishment I found an Eastern Pygmy-Possum curled up asleep in my rucksack. It was quite happy to pose for my camera when I released it among some banksia bushes.

One mammal frequently seen during daylight hours is the Echidna, which prefers the dry habitats of Freycinet. Normally solitary, it is a highly specialised feeder whose diet consists almost exclusively of ants.

The 6 km drive from Coles Bay to Cape Tourville offers outstanding views along the coast to the Friendly Beaches. There is an easy 20-minute circuit walk at Cape Tourville, and a viewing point that makes a great spot for seabird watching and gives excellent views to the Nuggets, offshore rocks which usually harbour roosting Black-faced Cormorants. Several seabirds breed on these islets including Little Penguin, Fairy Prion, White-faced Storm Petrel, Short-tailed Shearwater, Black-faced Cormorant, Pacific Gull, Silver Gull and Caspian Tern. Other birds seen from the viewpoint include the Australasian Gannet, Short-tailed Shearwater, Giant Petrel, White-bellied Sea-Eagle, Crested Tern, and Shy, Wandering, Black-browed and Yellow-nosed Albatrosses.

Hooded Plover breeds regularly along the Friendly Beaches and great care should be taken here during the breeding season to avoid disturbing nesting birds.

## Eastern Pygmy-Possum
*Cercartetus nanus*

Widespread across much of Tasmania except the midlands agricultural areas, this nocturnal, agile climber feeds mainly on nectar and pollen, gathered with its brush-tipped tongue from eucalyptus, banksias and bottlebrushes. Spiders, moths, termites and beetles are also eaten. The Eastern Pygmy-Possum uses its long, prehensile tail, which is largely naked along most of its length, as an aid in climbing.

This minute marsupial is threatened by clear-felling of old-growth mature forest and the firewood industry, both of which destroy their nesting hollows.

## Masked Owl
*Tyto novaehollandiae*

Related to the Barn Owl, the Tasmanian variety of this powerful owl is considerably larger than the mainland race, and roosts by day in a cave or a hollow in a tree. Tasmanian Masked Owls have huge talons and prey on a wide variety of animals including potoroos, bandicoots, possums, rabbits, rats and mice, as well as small- to medium-sized birds such as starlings, magpies or kookaburras.

As Masked Owls are highly secretive, it is very difficult to see one in the wild.

Pied Oystercatcher and Red-capped Plover also occur.

For the reasonably fit person, a walk from the car park at Parsons Cove between the peaks of the Hazards to Wineglass Bay is recommended. This walk is about 6 km, or three to four hours return. It passes through dry sclerophyll woodland, and a variety of birds may be seen including Wedge-tailed Eagle, Brown Falcon, Yellow-tailed Black-Cockatoo, Green Rosella, Common Bronzewing, Fan-tailed Cuckoo (summer only), Laughing Kookaburra, Black-faced Cuckoo-Shrike (summer only), Dusky and Scarlet Robins, Grey Shrike-Thrush, Golden Whistler, Grey Fantail and Satin Flycatcher (summer only). Spotted Quail-Thrush is uncommon here but worth searching for. It spends most of its time on the ground. Also look for Superb Fairy-Wren, White-browed Scrubwren, Brown Thornbill, Yellow Wattlebird, Eastern Spinebill, Beautiful Firetail, Striated and Spotted Pardalotes, Silvereye, Dusky Woodswallow (spring and summer only), Grey Butcherbird, Grey Currawong, and New Holland, Crescent and Yellow-throated Honeyeaters. Tasmanian Native-Hen is also found near the campground, while the secretive Bassian Thrush frequents some of the darker, forested gullies.

## Spotted Quail-Thrush
*Cinclosoma puntatum*

The only quail-thrush to be found in Tasmania is an uncommon, elusive and wary bird. It is restricted to areas of dry sclerophyll woodland, particularly on rocky ridges where the ground is covered in a dense amount of leaf litter and other debris. The cryptic, mottled plumage of the Spotted Quail-Thrush makes it extremely well camouflaged in its stony habitat, where it is easily overlooked.

These ground-nesting birds could suffer a severe population decline if foxes become established in Tasmania. They may be seen at Freycinet National Park and other areas of suitable east coast habitat.

© Jim Napier

## Sugar Glider
*Petaurus breviceps*

This small, nocturnal possum is arboreal and able to glide up to 50 metres by spreading the membrane which extends along each side of its body from the first toe of its foot to the fifth finger of its fore limb.

The Sugar Glider is common throughout Tasmania wherever suitable habitat exists. It is suggested that landowners protect any old or dead trees that contain holes or hollows, as these are required by a variety of wildlife such as hole-nesting birds, bats, Sugar Gliders and other possums.

By spotlighting at night you may find a Tawny Frogmouth, Southern Boobook Owl or even a Tasmanian Masked Owl.

This dry area is also ideal habitat for reptiles including the Tiger Snake (venomous), Blotched Blue-Tongue, Mountain Dragon and White's Skink.

The brackish lagoons south of the Hazards do not usually hold many waterbirds, although Brown Quail may be seen.

Finally, the seas around Freycinet provide a safe harbour for several marine mammals. Common and Bottlenose Dolphin occur year-round; during winter and spring, migrating Humpback and Southern Right Whales are being seen more regularly. Australian Fur Seals breed on Isle des Phoques south of Schouten Island. ■

## Common Bronzewing
*Phaps chalcoptera*

This large, wary pigeon remains common throughout much of Tasmania wherever there is forest or scrub. The species has declined in agricultural areas due to clearing of its habitat, but does manage to hang on if areas of scrub or woodland are retained. Although Common Bronzewings were formerly shot, being considered a delicacy, they are now fully protected.

They are most active during early morning or late afternoon, when they forage for the seeds of native plants as well as some introduced weeds and wheat grains. They may be seen at many of the sites in this book with suitable habitat, but they are shy and spend much of the day on the ground under trees or bushes.

# The
# SOUTH-EAST

# 14 Lake Dulverton

Lake Dulverton is a shallow, modified wetlands area bordering the picturesque Midlands town of Oatlands. Protected as a wildlife sanctuary since 1929, the lake has a history of varying water levels. At one time there was a diving board at the now dry edge near the former Aquatic Club, and historic photos show cattle surrounded by floodwaters. Conversely, when the lake waters dried up in the 1990s, a former airstrip was revealed. In recent years the lake has largely been dry and the local community has undertaken works to help ensure water levels remain in a small section of the lake, creating an oasis for waterfowl.

Since the early 1990s there have been noticeable changes to Tasmania's wetlands. Traditionally, enough rain fell in winter to fill the wetlands and maintain them throughout the following summer.

However, rainfall patterns have changed, with drier winters and heavy rainfall in early summer. The water left from these summer storms evaporates quickly, leaving shallow wetlands, such as Lake Dulverton, dry for much of the year.

Changing weather patterns have also seen alterations in bird activity. For many years Lake Dulverton was the only site in Tasmania where the Great Crested Grebe had been recorded breeding. However, it is now more than a decade since this species has been recorded at the lake as the wetland habitat is no longer suitable due to lack of water. The species has, however, been recorded breeding at a few other Tasmanian locations.

The attractive Australasian Shoveler (opposite, top) has a bill that is especially adapted to feeding at the water's surface, where it sieves food while filtering water.

One of Tasmania's most common frogs, the Brown Tree Frog (above right) is widely distributed across Tasmania in a wide range of habitats except alpine areas.

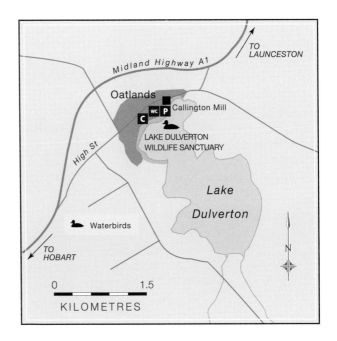

## Hoary-headed Grebe

*Poliochephalus poliocephalus*

This small grebe is endemic to Australia and has been introduced to New Zealand. It is a common grebe in Tasmania and may be seen on many large, open lagoons of brackish or fresh water. It normally breeds during spring following periods of rainfall; the floating nest is built of water plants and algae generally attached to the stems of emergent water plants. The Hoary-headed Grebe does sometimes nest colonially.

These grebes may be seen at Goulds Lagoon, Granton, Lake Dulverton, and the lagoon at Narawntapu National Park, as well as farm dams, particularly in the south-east. They can regularly be seen on either side of the causeway between Midway Point and Sorell.

## Access

The historic town of Oatlands is located 85 km north of Hobart and 115 km south of Launceston on the Midland Highway (A1), about an hour's drive from Hobart and an hour and a half from Launceston. The main road now bypasses the town, leaving it a quiet step aside from the bustle of the modern world.

If you don't have a car, the town is serviced by bus several times a day (less on weekends), and if you catch an early bus, you could break your journey and spend a few hours birdwatching and exploring the town before catching another bus later in the day.

Oatlands has the highest concentration of Georgian sandstone buildings in Australia, with 87 significant sandstone buildings in High Street alone. The historic Callington Mill is adjacent to the Lake Dulverton picnic area. Birdwatching here has a backdrop of history and old-world charm, and the town is reasonably flat, making it quite accessible for walking and cycling.

## Facilities

Lake Dulverton has wheelchair-accessible toilets, picnic sites, electric barbecues and a walking track. There is a roadside camping and caravan area beside the lake. Camping is free, with a maximum three-night stay.

Accommodation, tea rooms, cafes, fuel and other facilities are available in the town. A walking guide to the lake is available from the visitor centre in High Street.

## Wildlife

Bird activity is most concentrated near the picnic area on the Esplanade at the northern end of the town. You'll have no trouble finding this spot. In about 1930, the local council built a small retaining dam here to prevent the marshland drying out in summer. For many decades this dam ensured a water depth of between two and three metres.

However, drier periods in the 1990s saw the water levels diminish to almost nothing and in 1996 a small earth bund wall was constructed to create a 2.2 hectare mini-lake. Volunteers then laid a pipeline to pipe water to the site from the headwaters of the Blackman River, 17 km west of Oatlands. You'll see another bund wall out into the more distant part of the lake, which isolates a section of the lake for water storage.

A symphony of bird calls greets you at the picnic area: the beautiful trumpet-like calls of Black Swans, the quacking of a number of duck species, the shrill notes of the Eurasian Coot and the staccato notes of the Masked Lapwing. A flock of Mallard will soon appear at your feet, anticipating food.

Even with the two dams, the mini-lake is quite shallow. It is covered with strap weed, a plant with long, ribbon-like leaves floating over the surface of the water, benefiting the shallow-feeding species listed above. Feeding activity is greatest during the early morning and evening. However, with the reduced hours of daylight in late autumn and winter, birdwatchers can expect to see plenty of activity throughout the day.

## Australian Shelduck

*Tadorna tadornoides*

Sometimes called Mountain Duck, these handsome waterfowl prefer coastal swamps and brackish lakes, although they do sometimes fly considerable distances to drink at freshwater lakes. Several times I have even come across small groups or pairs of Australian Shelduck resting on the surface of the sea several hundred metres from shore.

These large ducks feed essentially by grazing on water plants such as sedges, algae and duckweed, as well as grasses and clover. They also consume a range of insects and their larvae.

As well as Lake Dulverton, they may be seen at Narawntapu National Park, Moulting Lagoon, Orielton Lagoon and Cape Portland in the far north-east.

## Masked Lapwing

*Vanellus miles*

This common lapwing was previously called Spur-winged Plover and its strident chattering call is often heard throughout open and farmed areas of Tasmania, frequently at night. The Masked Lapwing is one of the few birds to have benefited from land clearing as they have been able to exploit the increased use of land by humans. I have even seen them nesting on roundabouts on busy main roads!

The Masked Lapwing is a fairly sedentary bird, particularly while breeding, although it does wander and form flocks outside of the breeding season.

As in many places, Mallard are becoming a pest. There is a mix of pure-bred Mallard and hybrids, resulting from breeding between domestic ducks and Pacific Black Duck. In high human-contact areas such as this, where persistent begging is rewarded with food, Mallard build in numbers, contaminating habitat and competing with native ducks for food. Please ignore their pleas to be fed.

A walk, or even a slow drive, around the lake might show you some other species, depending on water levels. The Great Crested Grebe once bred in the vicinity of the Aquatic Club. This small wetlands area can potentially contain some very interesting migrants depending on the season and water levels.

Previously, when water levels were higher, Eurasian Coot regularly nested here. Although it is a common bird it only rarely breeds in Tasmania. Black Swan and some duck species sometimes breed here, although breeding is difficult to predict as it is often associated with rain and the resultant rise in water levels.

Other bird species to be seen here (depending on water levels) are Australian Shelduck, Chestnut Teal, Australasian Shoveler, Hoary-headed Grebe and Double-banded and Red-capped Plovers. Whistling Kite has been recorded and Tiger Snakes are sometimes seen.

The quiet listener will often be rewarded with the calls of some of Tasmania's eleven frog species, such as Eastern Banjo Frog, Spotted Marsh Frog or Brown Tree Frog. ■

© Rob Blakers

# 15 Maria Island National Park

Proclaimed in 1972, Maria Island is another of Tasmania's spectacular national parks. Like Bruny Island, Maria consists of two large islands joined by a narrow isthmus. It has a rich tapestry of history, as well as being a haven for wildlife, and is the only national park in Tasmania where you can find all twelve of the state's endemic birds.

In the years 1969–71 several animal species were considered to be at risk on the Tasmanian mainland. Creatures such as the Forester Kangaroo, Tasmanian Bettong and Cape Barren Goose were then relocated to Maria Island as part of an effort to conserve them. Managing these 'introduced' species has brought challenges and ethical dilemmas due to the build up of unnaturally high populations.

While a long summer's day spent on the island will allow you to see most of the areas around the

## KEY SPECIES

- Bottlenose Dolphin
- Common Dolphin
- Forester Kangaroo
- Tasmanian Native-Hen
- Cape Barren Goose
- Hooded Plover
- Pied Oystercatcher
- Swift Parrot
- Forty-spotted Pardalote
- Blotched Blue-Tongue

township of Darlington, an overnight stay is recommended for the best wildlife-viewing opportunities.

## Access

Unless you are lucky enough to have your own plane or boat you'll need to take the passenger ferry from the wharf at the town of Triabunna, or charter a plane or boat to reach the island. No cars are allowed on the island but you can bring your bicycle.

Triabunna is about a one and a half hour drive from Hobart on the Tasman Highway (A3) via Sorell. From Launceston it's about a two and a half hour drive via Campbell Town and Swansea.

The passenger ferry travels seven days a week, but services may be interrupted in rough seas. For timetables and bookings phone 0428 666 650.

Information on boat and plane charters is available from the Triabunna Visitor Information Centre. Phone (03) 6257 4772 or email triabunna@tasvisinfo.com.au.

## Facilities

The island has three main camping areas; sites should be booked in advance. There is also basic accommodation in the old penitentiary. This convict building has bunk beds, mattresses, wood heaters and showers, but guests need to bring all their own bedding, food and a cooking stove.

There are gas barbecues, picnic shelters, flush toilets, drinking water, public phones and many walking tracks on the island.

The historic Commissariat Store building near the jetty has visitor information and, in busy periods, a Parks and Wildlife Service officer is based there. Call in to gather information on the walking tracks, wildlife, camping, bicycle code and the island's fascinating history.

## Wildlife

Your wildlife experience begins on the ferry trip to the island across Mercury Passage, so have your binoculars ready. Short-tailed Shearwaters can often be seen

## FORESTER KANGAROO
### *Macropus giganteus*

The Forester Kangaroo is Tasmania's largest native land mammal. It is common in only a few select areas and, being predominantly a grazing animal, prefers open grassy plains, dry sclerophyll forests and grassy woodlands.

The Forester Kangaroo was almost wiped out during the early twentieth century and is now regularly found only in the far north-east (Mt William National Park), the mid-north coast (Narawntapu National Park) and areas of the Midlands plains. It is also commonly seen on Maria Island, where it has been introduced.

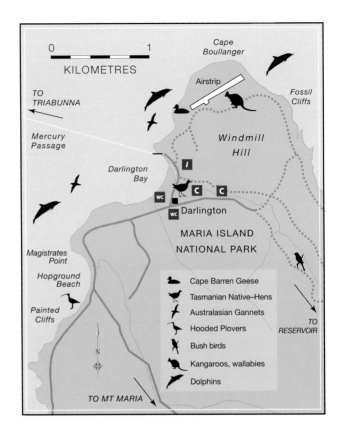

on the water, both flying and diving or settled in 'rafts', and Australasian Gannets are commonly seen. During stormy weather Shy Albatross often visit the passage. Common and Bottlenose Dolphins also often delight ferry passengers.

Besides being a national park, Maria Island is also a marine reserve, and a large number of fish can be seen from the jetty at Darlington. If you're able to take a wetsuit and snorkel, this is a wonderful place for enjoying underwater wildlife.

The cluster of historic buildings at Darlington generally beckons visitors first

and is a good place to start touring Maria Island. As you wander around you'll have plenty of opportunities to see Cape Barren Geese and Tasmanian Native-Hens up close. If you're staying overnight you can expect a rather raucous dawn 'chorus' from these locals, both of which were introduced to the island. In spring and summer Welcome Swallows flit in and out of the old buildings where they have easily visible nests.

Forester Kangaroo and Bennett's Wallaby can often be seen around the old penitentiary quadrangle, but to see large groups of these macropods a walk to the

## Swift Parrot

*Lathamus discolor*

During summer Swift Parrots are reasonably common in the drier areas of the state, preferring forests containing Blue Gums. Like Lorikeets, Swift Parrots are nectar feeders and their brush-tipped tongue aids in collecting nectar from eucalypt blossoms. Swift Parrots breed only in Tasmania and migrate to the south-east Australian mainland for the winter.

This fast-flying parrot is decreasing due to destruction of its forest habitat and a diminishing number of suitable hollows for nesting. Tasmania's firewood industry is partly to blame for cutting down old or dead trees with hollows that take at least 100 years to form.

Swift Parrots may be seen (during spring) at Mt Wellington, Tinderbox Peninsula, Bruny Island, Maria Island and Launceston's Cataract Gorge.

airstrip is suggested. The Forester Kangaroo is the Tasmanian sub-species of the Eastern Grey Kangaroo. Before 1969, the Tasmanian Pademelon and the Long-nosed Potoroo were the only macropods on the island. Besides being smaller, these animals are also not as outgoing or conspicuous as their larger relatives. Your best chances of seeing them are in the damp forest areas, such as the Reservoir Track, particularly at dawn and dusk.

Tasmanian Blue Gums are widespread on the island. In spring and early summer their blossoms provide the key food source for the Swift Parrot, which nests on the island. If they're about, these slender bright-green parrots make themselves known. They chatter constantly while feeding and, as per their name, fly swiftly while calling to each other.

Many wildlife lovers are attracted to Maria Island in the hope of seeing some of Tasmania's endemic birds. In total over 120 species of birds have been recorded here. Green Rosellas can be readily seen and heard as they are quite common on Maria Island. With a little effort, most birdwatchers should also be able to see the Strong-billed and Black-headed Honeyeaters. These feed in noisy flocks on eucalypt trees, both species often feeding together— particularly in autumn and winter. It's often the sound of bark being ripped off trees that gives away the presence of flocks of Strong-billed Honeyeaters as they poke into tree crevices to find bugs, ants, beetles and other food. The Black-headed Honeyeaters feed in similar forest, but in the middle to higher sections of the tree, where they gather insects from leaves. The eucalypt trees on the Reservoir Track are good places to watch and listen for these species.

More elusive endemics are the Forty-spotted Pardalote and the Scrubtit, both of which can be seen near the reservoir. Try to observe the differences in the eucalypt trees and this will help you find the Forty-spotted Pardalote. Its favoured feeding tree is the Manna or White Gum, which occur near the reservoir. Once you've found these trees, look high up in the tree canopy where the Forty-spotted Pardalotes feed, gleaning sugary sap from the leaves. Most feed constantly in the same group of trees so, with patience, you will see them here. It will help if you can familiarise yourself with their call. Powerful binoculars may be needed to see them, and a raincoat or the like is suggested so you can lie on the ground and look up into the trees.

Other birds to be seen along the Reservoir Track include the Crescent Honeyeater, Beautiful Firetail, Scrubtit, Tasmanian and Brown Thornbills and that regular chatterbox, the Tasmanian Scrubwren. Olive Whistler and Grey Shrike-Thrush can be readily heard, and you might see a Bassian Thrush foraging on the ground. Tree Martins fly constantly

## Pied Oystercatcher
*Haematopus longirostris*

This brightly coloured, plump wader is very much a feature of Tasmanian beaches and estuaries. The Pied Oystercatcher is a sociable bird and is commonly seen resting in groups on sand bars when not breeding. Territories are defended year-round when pairs or small groups become quite vocal, frequently giving long, piping trills.

Unfortunately the increased use of beaches by humans has resulted in a lower breeding success. Pied Oystercatchers are now unable to nest on some beaches due to this pressure. As these birds do not commence breeding until seven years of age, a decline in population may not be evident for some years, by which time it may be too late.

**111**

## Shy Albatross
*Diomedea cauta*

This large mollymawk is the only albatross to breed in Australian waters. The Shy (or White-capped) Albatross breeds on remote, windswept islands such as Albatross Island, a few kilometres north-west of Hunter Island in the state's north-west, and Mewstone and Pedra Branca off southern Tasmania.

The Shy Albatross rarely follows ships except fishing vessels, but does frequently fly close to the coast, particularly during bad weather.

In Tasmania it is most easily seen on the ferry crossing of Mercury Passage to Maria Island, or from pelagic boat trips leaving from Eaglehawk Neck on the Tasman Peninsula or Port Arthur.

Unfortunately the Shy Albatross is declining in number due to long-line fishing. Many albatrosses become impaled on the long-line hooks while attempting to swallow bait. Many albatrosses are also killed after ingesting pieces of plastic floating in the ocean that they have mistaken for food.

over the reservoir. Scan the sky, as a Wedge-tailed Eagle may be seen soaring above.

Both Hooded Plovers and Pied Oystercatchers breed on Darlington and Hopground Beach. These birds have the most vulnerable 'nests'—a mere scrape in the sand. Walk on the wet sand and keep your eyes peeled for clusters of about three eggs in dry sand, sometimes barely a metre above the high-tide line. I remember the joy and alarm I had one day with some birdwatching friends when we happened across a Hooded Plover's nest on Hop-ground Beach. An overnight Rogaine event (cross-country walking and navigation) was to occur there that very night. We headed straight back and lobbied the ranger to have the beach declared 'off bounds' for the event, to which he agreed.

A longer walk to the Fossil Cliffs yields views of Bird Rock, its white markings showing it as a favoured roosting place for seabirds. White-bellied Sea-Eagles can often be seen soaring high above the cliffs and Peregrine Falcons may possibly be seen.

Tasmania's three snake species all reside here so robust footwear is essential. If staying overnight, you can readily see various species of small bats flying at dusk, in all but the coldest weather.

Several species of lizard are to be found, including Tasmania's largest lizard, the Blotched Blue Tongue. This slow-moving lizard is a member of the skink family and is the most cold-adapted member of its genus.

## Tree Martin
*Hirundo nigricans*

This migratory martin is common across much of Tasmania wherever there is suitable habitat. Tree Martins prefer larger eucalypts—usually near water—with hollows in which they can nest, often in loose colonies. They frequently feed over water, in mixed flocks with Welcome Swallows, particularly at the end of the breeding season before departing north to the Australian mainland.

Tree Martins are graceful fliers with long, pointed wings and a short but broad bill that is perfectly adapted for catching insects while in flight. They may be seen at Narawntapu and Maria Island National Parks.

# 16 Derwent Valley and Goulds Lagoon

The Derwent River is a magnificent wetland habitat right on Hobart's doorstep, although precious little is reserved except Goulds Lagoon.

## Access

By taking the main road north of Hobart (the A1) and continuing through the northern suburbs for almost 20 km you arrive at a long bridge over the Derwent River at the village of Granton. Turn left off the main road, just before the bridge, onto the Lyell Highway (A10), signed New Norfolk. Here there is a large car park close to a superb area for waterfowl.

To reach Goulds Lagoon, drive south from Granton on the A1 and take the first left turn for Austins Ferry. After about 3 km you will pass Goulds Lagoon on the right-hand side of the road. Turn right just past the lagoon and you will see a small car park on your right.

## Facilities

There is a car park at Granton. At Goulds Lagoon there is a small car park and bird hide.

## Wildlife

The main interest here is the birdlife, although some whales and dolphins may sometimes be seen in the Derwent estuary south-east of Hobart. In fact, during the last century, residents of Hobart and Sandy Bay living close to the river frequently complained of lack of sleep due to the Southern Right Whales cavorting in the estuary! Unfortunately the whaling industry soon decimated this population

Hoary-headed Grebes often nest in small groups on the water's surface. They feed on a variety of prey such as zoo plankton or aquatic insects obtained by diving.

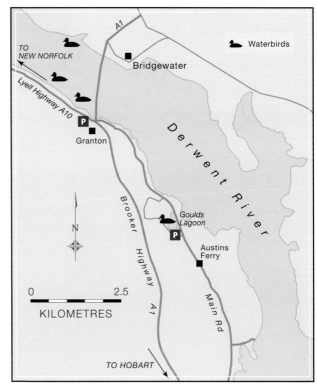

The common Eastern Banjo Frog (opposite) is often known as a 'Pobblebonk' due to its well-known call, which is a series of musical plonks reminiscent of a banjo.

115

## Brown Falcon
*Falco berigora*

This is a very common falcon in Tasmania, where it is frequently seen perched by the side of roads. It has a fairly leisurely flight, with slow wingbeats; when gliding the wings are held in a shallow 'V'. The Tasmanian Brown Falcon has a darker plumage than the pale-coloured form on the Australian mainland.

The Brown Falcon is primarily a bird of open country that has adapted well to agricultural areas. Its diet consists of small mammals such as mice or young rabbits, with some lizards, snakes and small birds. A wide variety of invertebrates are also eaten including crickets, grasshoppers, beetles and other insects. It is widespread across most of Tasmania and is frequently highly vocal.

of whales, which is now slowly increasing again due to protection.

### Granton
The best site for watching waterfowl is undoubtedly just upstream from Granton. There are often huge numbers of Black Swan, hundreds of Chestnut Teal, together with Pacific Black Duck, Grey Teal, Australian Shelduck, Australasian Shoveler and the bizarre Musk Duck. Look carefully and you may find Hardhead and on rare occasions, a Blue-billed Duck. Great Cormorant sometimes breed here if there are flood-washed trees in the river on which to build nests. Little Pied and Little Black Cormorant as well as Eurasian Coot and Hoary-headed Grebe are also usually seen here.

North of the river are large areas of reed beds and marshes which are frequented by Swamp Harrier, Tasmanian Native-Hen,

Purple Swamphen, White-faced Heron, Great Egret (winter only), Lewin's Rail, Spotless Crake, Latham's Snipe (summer only), Clamorous Reed-Warbler (summer only), White-fronted Chat and Little Grassbird. Rarely, Australasian Bittern (it may possibly breed) and Baillon's Crake may be seen.

## Goulds Lagoon

This small conservation area is managed by Glenorchy Council and can produce many interesting birds, even if dry during summer. It was declared a wildlife sanctuary in 1938, and recently proclaimed a nature conservation area.

The fringing reed beds are attractive to nesting Black Swan, Tasmanian Native-Hen, Clamorous Reed-Warbler and Little Grassbird. The lagoon is probably at its best as the water recedes during early summer, when the muddy margins attract crakes and rails as well as several species of duck.

Approximately 60 bird species have been recorded for this small ephemeral lagoon, including Hoary-headed Grebe, Chestnut Teal, Grey Teal, Pacific Black Duck, Hardhead, Australasian Shoveler, Brown Falcon, Great and Little Pied Cormorants, Purple Swamphen, Eurasian Coot, Cattle Egret, Great Egret, White-faced Heron and Australian Spotted Crake. Even a Little Ringed Plover has been seen at this site.

Four frog species have been recorded: Brown Froglet, Spotted Marsh Frog, Eastern Banjo Frog and Brown Tree Frog.

## Great Cormorant
*Phalacrocorax carbo*

Tasmania's largest cormorant feeds on a large variety of fish, insects and crustaceans, which it catches by diving underwater for periods of up to one minute or more. It usually inhabits coastal bays and estuaries as well as large rivers and inland lakes.

At the onset of breeding, the adults develop white flank patches and a crest on the rear of the head. In Tasmania, nests are often placed on dead trees or stumps in the water of lagoons or large rivers, such as near Granton on the Derwent River.

# 17 Mt Wellington

## KEY SPECIES

- Dusky Antechinus
- Tasmanian Pademelon
- Yellow-tailed Black-Cockatoo
- Green Rosella
- Yellow-throated Honeyeater
- Strong-billed Honeyeater
- Black-headed Honeyeater
- Scrubtit
- Black Currawong
- Ocellated Skink

At 1270 metres, Mt Wellington dominates the city of Hobart. Holding sway over more than the view, it has a strong influence on the city's weather, and for many locals is a source of inspiration in their daily lives. Besides its impressive towering dolerite pinnacles and varied colours, the mountain has an array of vegetation communities which house a diversity of wildlife, including about 60 bird species. Ten of Tasmania's endemic species can be readily found while walking on Mt Wellington. Most of the natural areas of Mt Wellington have now been included in a large park called Wellington Park, which covers an area of over 18,250 hectares.

## Access

Mt Wellington is easily accessible from the city by car or bus. Those with more time could walk or cycle from the city. There are a range of tracks allowing for short, easy rambles to long, energetic day walks and everything in between.

Being an altitudinal migrant, the endemic Black Currawong (opposite) keeps to the high mountains of mainland Tasmania during summer.

To access Mt Wellington, drive south-west via Davey Street and the Huon Road (B64) towards Fern Tree. Drivers need to be in the right-hand lane driving up Davey Street, otherwise you will be forced to take the Southern Outlet to Kingston. Buses run from Franklin Square in Macquarie Street and operate frequently during the week, with less frequent services on weekends. Timetables can be checked with Metro Tasmania (phone 132 201 or see www.metrotas.com.au).

If you are walking, make your way through South Hobart to the Waterworks Reserve at the top of Waterworks Road in

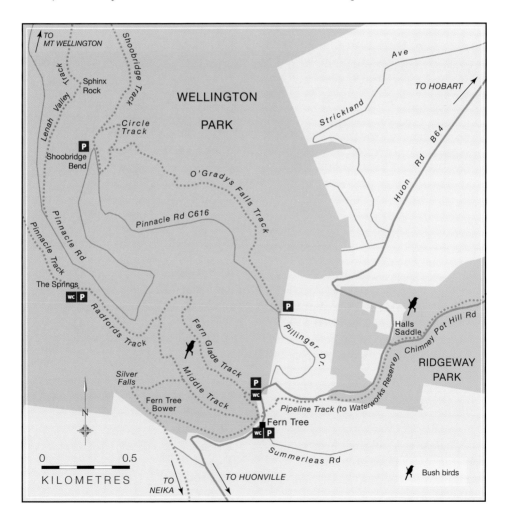

The inquisitive Dusky Antechinus remains common in areas of suitable habitat across much of Tasmania, where it forages for soil invertebrates and sometimes berries.

Dynnyrne. At the far end of the reserve take the Pipeline Track via the dry Gentle Annie Falls. You can follow this track all the way to Fern Tree. An alternative to walking is to catch the bus to Fern Tree and return to Hobart on foot.

### Halls Saddle

Here the Pipeline Track crosses Chimney Pot Hill Road near bus stop 25. From here it's a 30–40 minute walk to the Waterworks Reserve, and a 15–20 minute walk to Fern Tree.

### Fern Glade Track

This commences just after you pass the road to Mt Wellington (C616). There's a car park in a disused quarry. If travelling by bus, alight at bus stop 26 almost opposite the car park, or stop 27 (Fern Tree) and walk back on the track behind the historic St Raphael's Church.

### Fern Tree

There is car parking in Stephenson Place. If it is full, return to the quarry at the Fern Glade Track. If travelling by bus, alight at bus stop 27.

### Shoobridge Bend

This is a sharp, U-shaped bend on the Pinnacle Road (C616) about 1.6 km after leaving the houses in Pillinger Drive. It is not signposted, but there is a small car park on the left and a road safety sign indicating a steep bend. For walkers, the *Mount Wellington Walk Map and Notes* shows the tracks that lead here.

### The Springs

From Shoobridge Bend, continue up the Pinnacle Road about another 1.5 km. A number of walking tracks end at the Springs and new ones take off from here. You could walk to the Springs from Fern Tree and return via another track, but for your safety you do need the above map.

## Facilities

Halls Saddle has a picnic shelter and wood barbecue.

Fern Glade Track is a walking track close to facilities at Fern Tree.

Fern Tree has toilets, picnic shelters, wood barbecues, several walking tracks, a shop and tavern.

Shoobridge Bend has walking tracks.

At the Springs there are toilets, picnic shelters, wood barbecues and several walking tracks.

## Wildlife

Halls Saddle is indicative of Mt Wellington, with two very different habitat types quite close together. The Pipeline Track heading to the Waterworks Reserve is open eucalypt forest with a prolific number of flowers in spring. The walk is relatively level for about 20 minutes and here you could see the endemic Yellow-throated, Strong-billed and Black-headed Honeyeaters, as well as Green Rosella. On misty days the Black Currawong might be here. The Grey Currawong has a 'clink clink' call that has given rise to its local name ('Clinking Currawong') and is often seen here. The calls of this bird are quite different to the Grey Currawong on mainland Australia, and its colour is darker.

In spring and summer the area is a concerto with the calls of many species that have spent winter on mainland Australia. Fan-tailed, Pallid and Horsfield's Bronze-Cuckoos can all be heard, as well as Spotted and Striated Pardalotes and Black-faced Cuckoo-shrike.

Heading towards Fern Tree from Halls Saddle, the track leads through closed, wet, shrubby forest with a eucalypt over-storey. It's good habitat for Bassian Thrush, Olive Whistler and also Long-

## White Goshawk

*Accipiter novaehollandiae*

This powerful and aggressive hunter occurs in two colour forms, a grey form and a pure-white form. Only the white form occurs in Tasmania, where it is widespread in forested areas of the state. As with other accipiters, the female is considerably larger than the male.

The White Goshawk is a difficult bird to see in the wild, although forested areas in the north-west of Tasmania probably offer the best chance.

In Tasmania, this bird is usually referred to as a White Goshawk even though officially its name is the Grey Goshawk.

© Jim Napier

## Forest Raven
*Corvus tasmanicus*

Mainland Tasmania's only member of the raven family is widespread across the state and is found in a wide range of habitats. It is the largest of all the ravens, with a characteristic deep cawing which resounds through the woodlands and scrub.

Similar to most members of the crow family, Forest Ravens are omnivorous and able to exploit a range of food resources including insects, carrion, fruits of native and introduced plants, and eggs and nestlings of birds. Outside the breeding season they roam the countryside in loose, nomadic flocks.

nosed Potoroo. Where the historic aqueducts cross the moist fern gullies, watch for Tasmanian Thornbill and Pink Robin.

The Dusky Antechinus or Dusky Marsupial Mouse, although rarely seen, is quite common in these forests.

The Fern Glade Track is another cool, moist, shady area that is good habitat for Tasmanian Scrubwren and Scrubtit. Both endemics, the Tasmanian Scrubwren lives in low shrubs and is easy to find as it makes its 'cranky little sounds' when walkers approach, whereas the Scrubtit is more elusive and behaves like a treecreeper. It has a white eye-ring and a white throat and upper breast. With some patience, you will see it as it's locally common. You can look for the Scrubtit and Pink Robin in the dense stands of tree ferns, where the Fern Glade track follows Longhill Creek. Tasmanian Pademelon could be seen here during the day. Watch for fallen trees that have been ripped to pieces by Yellow-tailed Black-Cockatoos in search of grubs. These raucous and spectacular birds are often heard screeching above.

From Fern Tree you can walk further along the Pipeline Track for as little or as far as you like, as the track goes a further 12 km from Fern Tree. However, a nice option is to walk as far as Neika (about 4.3 km from Fern Tree). If you're able to walk this track in the evening, Eastern Barred Bandicoots can be seen towards the Neika end. Tawny Frogmouth can often be seen roosting in tall eucalypts in the vicinity of the junction to Silver Falls. Take the time to look upwards and scan the branches.

At Shoobridge Bend, the Circle Track provides a short loop walk through closed, wet forest where Brown and Tasmanian Thornbills might be seen. There are some large gum-topped stringybarks and hollows in tall eucalypts on Mt Wellington which are used as nests by numerous species including Swift Parrot, Green Rosella and Yellow-tailed Black-Cockatoo.

Notice the bleached remains of dead trees and stumps from the disastrous 1967 bush fires. Although these giants have been dead for many years, they do provide a wonderful habitat for many species of mammals, birds and reptiles as well as a multitude of insects. Unfortunately dead trees are usually undervalued and only seen as a source of cheap firewood. Nothing could be further from the truth as dead wood, whether standing or lying on the ground, is vital for maintaining diversity of animal life in our woodlands and forests. A recent Birds Australia study has shown that bird diversity increases by 30 per cent for every ten large, old or dead trees left standing.

A longer and more challenging walk at Shoobridge Bend is to follow the Shoobridge Track to where it meets the Lenah Valley Track, then turn left and follow the Lenah Valley Track back past Rock Cabin and descend back to the Shoobridge Track on the track that passes

## Tasmanian Pademelon
*Thylogale billardierii*

A medium-sized wallaby, the Tasmanian Pademelon at present remains widespread and common— even abundant—in some areas across much of the state. It prefers the dense vegetation of rainforests, Tea-Tree scrub and heathland, as well as drier woodlands where damp gullies or patches of dense vegetation exist.

Tasmanian Pademelons are easily seen at many of the sites in this book including Narawntapu, Mt William and Cradle Mountain–Lake St Clair National Parks.

## Scarlet Robin
*Petroica multicolour*

This small, plump robin is common and widespread across Tasmania and may be seen in a variety of habitats. During the breeding season Scarlet Robins inhabit eucalypt forests and woodlands, but disperse into more open country during autumn and winter, when they frequently visit parks and gardens.

Scarlet Robins begin breeding during late winter when the female builds a cup nest of fine bark strips, grasses and moss, frequently camouflaged with scraps of lichen or bark. Several cuckoo species are known to parasitise Scarlet Robin nests.

via the base of Sphinx Rock. Then retrace your steps back to Shoobridge Bend. This walk will give you a greater variety of habitat, including crossing a boulder field where lizards such as the Metallic and Ocellated Skinks can be seen in warmer weather. Expect to hear the melodious call of the Grey Shrike-Thrush and the plaintive call of the Dusky Robin. Scarlet Robin, Yellow-Throated Honeyeater and Green Rosella can also be seen here.

You can also start the Lenah Valley Track at the Springs and walk as far as perhaps Rock Cabin or Lone Cabin and then retrace your steps to the Springs. This is a reasonably level option, allowing you to enjoy similar species as described above. However, remember that while the car park is only a short distance away, you are now over 700 metres above sea level and cold, wet weather can develop at any time. Please ensure you have adequate clothing if walking from here.

Other birds to look out for on any of the tracks are Wedge-tailed Eagle (soaring above), White Goshawk, Crescent Honeyeater, Golden Whistler, Spotted and Striated Pardalotes, Flame and Scarlet Robins, Forest Raven and Black Currawong.

In suitable weather, the Springs is a pleasant site for picnicking, gentle rambling and bird watching. This is the beauty of Mt Wellington: there's a range of options for enjoying the environment, the wildlife and the glorious views.

# 18 The Botanical Gardens and Queens Domain

In 1818 the Royal Tasmanian Botanical Gardens were established as the gardens of Government House in Hobart. These magnificent gardens are situated in the Queens Domain on the right bank of the Derwent River and cover 13.5 hectares. Although many of the plants, trees and shrubs are exotics, a good range of native bird species can usually be seen.

Immediately west of the gardens is the Queens Domain—an area of open, grassy woodland with interesting bird life, classified as a reserve.

## Access

The Botanical Gardens and Queens Domain are located 2 km north of the Hobart city centre, near the Tasman Bridge. Take the Tasman Highway north from Hobart, then just past the Aquatic Centre (on your left) turn left into

The iconic Peregrine Falcon is one of the world's fastest birds. A supreme predator, it eats mainly avian prey, which it kills in flight following a breathtaking chase.

## KEY SPECIES

- Musk Lorikeet
- Swift Parrot
- Eastern Rosella
- Laughing Kookaburra

Lower Domain Road. The Botanical Gardens will be seen on your right.

## Facilities

The Botanical Gardens has car parking, a visitor centre and shop, wheelchair-accessible toilets, restaurant and kiosk. Entry is free and the gardens are open daily from 8.00 a.m.

The only facilities at Queens Domain are car parking plus walking tracks.

## Wildlife

### Botanical Gardens

Most botanical gardens are pleasant venues that also happen to be enticing to a range of bird species. Hobart's delightful and well laid out Botanical Gardens attract a diverse variety of easily seen species. The small lake attracts Pacific Black Duck and White-faced Heron, which also forages on the lawns. The ubiquitous Silver Gull is common, as are Green and Eastern Rosellas. Other birds reported include the following summer visitors: Tree Martin, Welcome Swallow, Swift Parrot, Black-faced Cuckoo-Shrike, Striated Pardalote and Silvereye. Residents to be seen all year include the Masked Lapwing, Laughing Kookaburra, Yellow and Little Wattlebirds, Yellow-throated, New Holland and Crescent Honeyeaters, Eastern Spinebill, Grey Fantail, Superb Fairy-Wren and Yellow-rumped and Brown Thornbills; Musk Lorikeets are sometimes attracted to the flowering eucalypts.

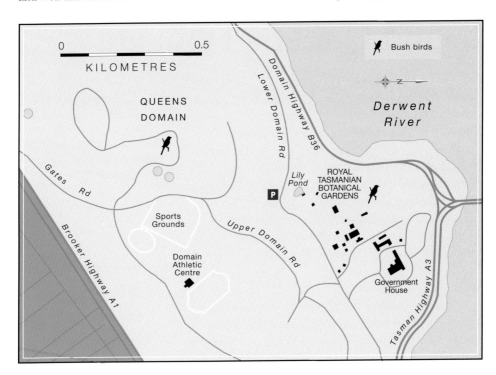

## Black-faced Cuckoo-Shrike
*Coracina novaehollandiae*

Although these well-known summer migrants are neither cuckoos nor shrikes, they do superficially resemble cuckoos with their slender shape, and their bills are shrike-like.

Black-faced Cuckoo-Shrikes build characteristic shallow, flimsy nests on a branch usually quite high in a tree (up to 20 metres). They are easily recognised in flight by their long and graceful undulations; when alighting they repeatedly open and close their wings.

Black-faced Cuckoo-Shrikes are quite widespread but restricted to wooded habitats, where they forage on a variety of insects and sometimes fruit.

127

## Eastern Rosella
*Platycercus eximus*

Nowhere near as common as the Green Rosella, this colourful bird, sometimes called the White-cheeked Rosella, is mainly confined to the eastern half of the state. This attractive parrot prefers drier, more open forests and is often seen in parks and gardens.

Although formerly more common, Eastern Rosellas have decreased considerably in recent years, no doubt due to lack of hollows for nesting, together with competition from the introduced European Starling for the limited number of hollows available.

The Eastern Rosella may be seen at Hobart's Botanical Gardens, the adjoining Domain area and Seven Mile Beach near Hobart Airport.

## Yellow Wattlebird
*Anthocaera paradoxa*

This largest of all honeyeaters is restricted to Tasmania and King Island, where it is common across most of the state, only being absent from parts of the far west. Yellow Wattlebirds are opportunistic feeders and after breeding gather in loose nomadic flocks to feed on nectar from blossoms, insects and spiders, as well as native and cultivated fruit.

This easily identified bird frequently visits parks and gardens and may be seen at many of the sites in this book.

## Queens Domain

This area of bushland is certainly worth a visit as it can harbour many of the bird species seen in the adjacent Botanical Gardens. Eastern Rosella and Australian Magpie are common here. Many species of raptor have also been recorded including the Australian Hobby, Brown Falcon, Brown and White Goshawks, Peregrine Falcon, Collared Sparrowhawk and Southern Boobook Owl.

If visiting early or late in the day you may spot Common Brushtail and Ringtail Possums and several species of bat.

Several lizards are known to occur including the Mountain Dragon, Metallic Skink, Blotched Blue-Tongue and the rare and threatened Tussock Grass Skink. ■

## Brown Goshawk
*Accipiter fasciatus*

This common bird of prey is secretive by nature, skulking within woodlands and silently moving from tree to tree to surprise its prey with a sudden attack. It eats a wide variety of prey, ranging from small- and medium-sized birds to mammals (up to the size of a rabbit), frogs, lizards and large insects.

The Brown Goshawk is widespread throughout Tasmania and may even be seen in wooded gardens in suburbs.

# 19

# Peter Murrell Reserve

## KEY SPECIES

- Platypus
- Tasmanian Bettong
- Eastern Barred Bandicoot
- Tasmanian Native-Hen
- Green Rosella
- Forty-spotted Pardalote
- Yellow Wattlebird
- Yellow-throated Honeyeater
- Strong-billed Honeyeater
- Black-headed Honeyeater
- Dusky Robin

This superb reserve on the outskirts of Kingston is well worth a visit, particularly to see several of Tasmania's endemic bird species. The reserve, which extends to over 270 hectares, was proclaimed in 1997 and named in honour of a former director of the state's Parks and Wildlife Service. The area is largely dry sclerophyll woodland, with two small lakes on the western boundary.

## Access

The reserve is approximately 20 minutes south of Hobart by car. From Hobart, drive south on the Southern Outlet (A6) to Kingston. Continue on the road towards Kettering until you reach a roundabout after passing the Australian Antarctic Division headquarters on your left. At this roundabout take the second exit, then take the next left turn onto Huntingfield Avenue. After about 500 metres you will see a large building on the left. Immediately after this building, turn left down a dirt track which leads to a grassy parking area.

FORTY-SPOTTED PARDALOTE

*Pardalotus quadragintus*

For a bird watcher, the Forty-spotted Pardalote (opposite) is one of Tasmania's most sought-after birds. It is one of Australia's rarest birds, with a population of no more than 3000 individuals, all restricted to Tasmania. This endangered species has declined considerably since Europeans first colonised Tasmania and is still threatened by destruction of its dry woodland habitat, mainly by clearing for agriculture and for firewood.

The Forty-spotted Pardalote has major colonies on Maria and Bruny Islands. It may also be seen at Peter Murrell Reserve and nearby Tinderbox Peninsula.

Penrhyn Pond and the nearby Heron Pond are ideal sites for watching a range of wildlife, including Platypus or Forty-spotted Pardalote in nearby Manna Gums.

## Facilities

A small car park and walking tracks only.

## Wildlife

The reserve is mainly noted for its birdlife and is without doubt the closest and easiest site to Hobart to see the Forty-spotted Pardalote.

Walking due south from the car park you arrive at Penrhyn Pond, which is ringed by large White or Manna Gums, *Eucalyptus viminalis*. This is the tree species favoured most by Forty-spotted Pardalotes. As these trees are tall and Forty-spots are tiny, ideally you do need to arrive early or late in the day when the sun is low in the sky to aid searching. A day with little wind is also preferable to allow you to hear their call: a soft, nasal,

© Rob Blakers

monotone, double-note 'whi-whi'. Endemic to Tasmania, the Forty-spotted Pardalote is an endangered species, with a population of between 2000 and 3000 individuals. The Manna Gum is the key to the survival of this diminutive gem. Manna Gums produce lerps or manna, which is a sugary, white coating seen on the leaves and exuded by sap-sucking insects called psyllids. This manna forms a major part of the Forty-spotted Pardalote diet.

The Forty-spotted Pardalote nests in a hollow, usually in a living or dead tree or stump, but sometimes in a hole in a bank or in the ground. Birds may be seen feeding in Manna Gums all year round.

Many of the usual dry woodland species can also be seen in the reserve including Brown Quail, Tasmanian Native-Hen, Green Rosella, Laughing Kookaburra, Superb Fairy-Wren, Pallid and Fan-tailed Cuckoos (summer only), Spotted, Striated and Forty-spotted Pardalotes, Yellow Wattlebird, honeyeaters such as the Yellow-throated, Strong-billed, Black-headed, Crescent

and New Holland Honeyeaters, the Eastern Spinebill, Scarlet and Dusky Robins, Black-faced Cuckoo-Shrike and Dusky Woodswallow (both summer only) and Australian Magpie and Grey Currawong.

A bonus at this site is a chance to see a Platypus in one of the small lakes. The Eastern Banjo Frog or 'pobble-bonk' may also be heard calling here.

If you are in the reserve at dusk you may hear the high-pitched twittering of a Common Ringtail Possum. Look near Penrhyn Pond, where there is usually a nest of this beautiful animal high in a bush or tree. This is also a good site to see a Tasmanian Pademelon or even an Eastern-barred Bandicoot or Tasmanian Bettong. ■

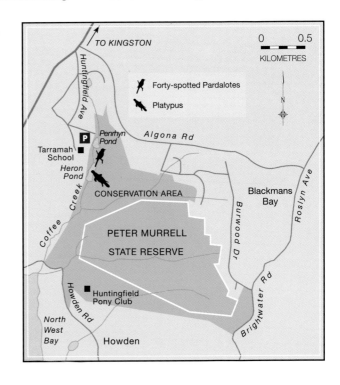

## Laughing Kookaburra
*Dacelo novaeguineae*

The well-known Laughing Kookaburra is the world's largest member of the kingfisher family and was introduced to Tasmania, where it is now quite common except in the wetter western areas. Kookaburras nest in holes in trees and usually lay two white eggs. They hunt by waiting patiently on a perch before flying to the ground to snatch their prey. Kookaburras eat a wide variety of animals such as insects, lizards, small snakes, small mammals and even birds.

The Laughing Kookaburra may be seen at Mt Nelson, Peter Murrell Reserve and nearby Tinderbox Peninsula, Freycinet Peninsula, Flinders Island or Cataract Gorge near Launceston.

## Striated Pardalote
*Pardalotus striatus*

This nomadic bird is the largest of all pardalotes and has several different races. Most Striated Pardalotes from Tasmania leave during autumn and migrate north across Bass Strait, where they may fly as far as Queensland in sometimes large, loose flocks.

Like other pardalotes, the Striated Pardalote builds a characteristic domed nest at the end of a burrow in the ground or in a bank, or in a hole in a tree. Four eggs are usually laid and extra birds often help to feed the chicks.

133

# 20

# Mt Nelson

## KEY SPECIES

- Eastern Barred Bandicoot
- Common Ringtail Possum
- Green Rosella
- Swift Parrot
- Tasmanian Scrubwren
- Yellow-throated Honeyeater
- Pink Robin
- Olive Whistler

Hobart's historic Mt Nelson Signal Station was built in 1811 to announce the arrival of boats in Storm Bay and is a fifteen-minute drive from the city centre. The lookout and adjacent restaurant offer superb views of the city and the Derwent estuary. Footpaths give access to areas of native bush that offer splendid opportunities for bird watching. The surrounding Truganini Reserve was declared in 1976 and extends to 65 hectares of mainly dry sclerophyll woodland.

**PALLID CUCKOO**
*Cuculus pallidus*

The solitary Pallid Cuckoo is fairly common across much of Tasmania, except parts of the west. This summer visitor does not build a nest, but lays a single egg in the nests of other species such as honeyeaters, Magpie Larks, flycatchers or cuckoo-shrikes. After hatching, the cuckoo nestling ejects the eggs or other nestlings from the nest.
  Pallid Cuckoos live on insects such as grasshoppers, beetles and hairy caterpillars.

## Access

You can choose from four different ways to reach Mt Nelson and return via the same route or a different one. This means you can mix-and-match your journey to make an interesting half-day trip.

Firstly, you can drive to the top. Take Sandy Bay Road as far as Wrest Point Hotel Casino, then take Mt Nelson Road, which leaves Sandy Bay Road directly opposite the turn-off into Wrest Point. The drive up to the reserve is easy to follow.

Secondly, you can catch the Metro bus up to Mt Nelson from Franklin Square in Macquarie Street, Hobart. Buses run frequently during the week, with less frequent services on weekends. Timetables can be checked with Metro Tasmania (phone 132 201 or see www.metrotas.com.au).

Thirdly, you can travel by car or bus and walk to the summit from Lambert Avenue (off Sandy Bay Road), Lambert Park and Bicentennial Park and onto Mt Nelson by a series of linked-up and easy to follow walking tracks. Buses can be taken from Franklin Square to Lambert Avenue (Stop 15) or to Churchill Avenue (Stop 17) to access the track at Bicentennial Park. It takes about 50 minutes to walk from Lambert Park, and about 30 minutes from Bicentennial Park. These are direct walking times only—wildlife watchers will take longer (and arrive less puffed!).

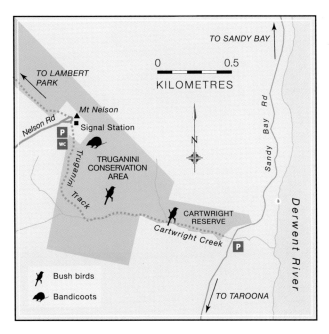

A fourth way is to travel by bus or car to the lower end of the Truganini Track (Stop 32) on Sandy Bay Road at Taroona. This track is about 45 minutes each way.

## Facilities

Mt Nelson has wheelchair-accessible toilets, picnic sites, electric barbecues and a restaurant in the historic Signal Station Cottage serving meals and refreshments throughout the day.

Dogs are permitted on leads in the Mt Nelson reserve, but not on the associated walking tracks.

## Wildlife

Once at the reserve, take a leisurely stroll down the Truganini Track to hear and observe birds of the dry forest environment. Birds to be seen here could

135

## Common Ringtail Possum
*Pseudocheirus peregrinus*

Strictly nocturnal, this attractive and variable possum remains common throughout Tasmania wherever there is suitable habitat. The long prehensile tail has a section of friction pad on the underside and is used as an extra hand to aid the animal while climbing among tree branches and bushes. It is also used to carry nesting material.

Common Ringtail Possums are frequently seen in gardens, even in suburbia, where they have adapted to eating a wide range of introduced leaves, flowers and fruit. To see them in the wild you will need to spotlight in suitable habitat, such as Tea-Tree thickets, at Melaleuca or Lake St Clair.

## Pink Robin
*Petroica rodinogaster*

Although widespread in Tasmania, the attractive Pink Robin is nowhere common and is restricted to particular types of habitat. Pink Robins usually inhabit shady areas of rainforest, wet fern gullies and Tea-Tree thickets, where established couples often occupy the same territories all year round.

As with most Australian robins, Pink Robins hunt by watching intently from a low perch and then diving onto their prey. Their diet consists largely of insects such as beetles, bugs and flies, as well as spiders. They may be seen at Mt Wellington, Mt Field National Park, Lake St Clair and Truganini Reserve, Hobart.

© Jim Napier

## Olive Whistler
*Pachycephala olivacea*

Although a widespread and common bird, Olive Whistlers are more often heard than seen. Their powerful whistling call is most often heard during spring and summer and is usually the only indication of the bird's presence. They prefer to remain under cover and are found in dense wet forests, coastal heathland, Tea-Tree forests and thickly vegetated parks and gardens.

This elusive bird is probably most easily seen at Melaleuca Inlet, and also occurs at Mt Wellington and Truganini Reserve and South Bruny, Maria Island and Mt Field National Parks.

## Beautiful Firetail
*Stagonopleura bella*

Tasmania is probably the stronghold of this stunning little finch, which is often seen in family parties or small groups, mainly during winter. During spring, pairs form to defend their breeding territory and roost together at night in a roost nest. Beautiful Firetails feed mainly on the ground on the seeds of various grasses and She-oaks, together with some insects.

Beautiful Firetails frequent woodlands, Tea-Tree scrub and coastal heathland from coastal areas to the mountains. Although these little finches may be seen at many of the sites in this book, they are particularly common at Melaleuca Inlet.

include six of Tasmania's endemics: Green Rosella, Dusky Robin, Yellow-throated and Black-headed Honeyeaters, Yellow Wattlebird and Tasmanian Scrubwren. Other birds occurring are the Swift Parrot (spring and early summer only), Fan-tailed and Pallid Cuckoos (summer only), Laughing Kookaburra, Striated Pardalote, Superb Fairy-Wren, Crescent and New Holland Honeyeaters, Eastern Spinebill, Scarlet and Flame Robins, Grey Shrike-Thrush, Satin Flycatcher, Grey Fantail, Brown Thornbill and Beautiful Firetail. Be sure to walk downhill as far as Cartwright Creek as the moist rainforest gully here provides opportunities for seeing Pink Robin and Olive Whistler.

As Tasmania's mammals are nocturnal you probably won't see them during the day. However, you may see evidence of their presence, such as scrapings in the bark of eucalypt trees caused by Common Ringtail or Common Brushtail Possums climbing, and plenty of conical holes dug by bandicoots in the open grassy lawns at the top of Mt Nelson.

If you're able to go to Mt Nelson at dusk, you will be rewarded with stunning views of the Derwent River—and if you're quiet and patient, you might sight an Eastern Barred Bandicoot or even a Tawny Frogmouth. Southern Boobook Owls may be heard calling, and the Tasmanian Masked Owl has also been recorded. ■

## 21 Sorell, Lauderdale and South Arm

Just a short drive east from Hobart in the vicinity of Sorell, Lauderdale and South Arm a number of shorebirds can be seen, including many migratory species that breed in the Arctic. Local species such as the Pied Oystercatcher and Hooded Plover are readily seen, but in this area they are increasingly competing for their habitat with dogs, roads, people and housing developments. Fortunately, in this area there are still large areas of valuable wetland habitats such as lagoons and coastal bays with large expanses of saltmarsh and mudflats.

### Access

The town of Sorell is easily reached from Hobart by travelling east on the Tasman Highway (A3). One birdwatching spot with public access is the causeway between Midway Point and Sorell (this is the second

Usually seen in ones or twos, the Greenshank (above) is a large migratory wader that breeds in the northern hemisphere near the Arctic circle.

### KEY SPECIES

- Pied Oystercatcher
- Hooded Plover
- Pacific Golden Plover
- Eastern Curlew
- Common Greenshank
- Bar-tailed Godwit

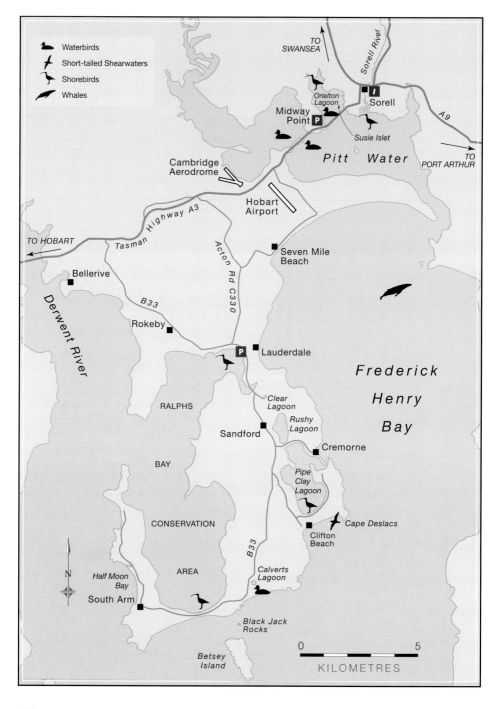

Waterbirds
Short-tailed Shearwaters
Shorebirds
Whales

TO SWANSEA

Sorell River

Orielton Lagoon

Midway Point P

Sorell

Susie Islet

Pitt Water

A9

TO PORT ARTHUR

Cambridge Aerodrome

Hobart Airport

Tasman Highway A3

TO HOBART

Acton Rd C330

Seven Mile Beach

Bellerive

B33

Rokeby

P Lauderdale

Frederick

Henry

Bay

RALPHS

Clear Lagoon

Rushy Lagoon

Sandford

Cremorne

BAY

Pipe Clay Lagoon

CONSERVATION

Cape Deslacs

Clifton Beach

N

AREA

B33

Half Moon Bay

Calverts Lagoon

South Arm

Black Jack Rocks

Betsey Island

Derwent River

0    5

KILOMETRES

One of our commonest bats is the Lesser Long-eared Bat, which is widespread across most of Tasmania in all forest types.

causeway as you drive east from Hobart). There is a small car park on the causeway, as well as a walking and cycling track, so you could park at Midway Point and walk across, allowing you to focus on the birds rather than the traffic.

Once across the causeway, take the first turn left into Nash Street, follow this and turn left into Forcett Street. Park at the end of this street (in the vicinity of the historic cemetery) and then walk the short distance to Orielton Lagoon.

There are two ways to reach Lauderdale and South Arm. The most direct route is to drive north from Hobart up the Tasman Highway (A3) towards Sorell and turn off at the Seven Mile Beach exit. Follow the road towards Seven Mile Beach, but turn off to Lauderdale when indicated with a sign. From this point Acton Road (C330) leads to Lauderdale.

The alternative route is to cross the Tasman Bridge (A3) and take the exit to Bellerive. From Bellerive, take road B33 to Rokeby and Lauderdale.

## Facilities

Public toilets are located at Sorell, Clifton Beach Surf Life Saving Club and South Arm Marina.

Food and fuel can be purchased at Sorell, Lauderdale and South Arm and a visitor information centre is located at Sorell.

## Wildlife

Great Crested Grebes can be seen on either side of the causeway between Midway Point and Sorell. However, the northern side of the causeway (Orielton Lagoon) has safer options for pedestrians. In breeding season, Great Crested Grebes are unmistakeable with their pointed black ear-tufts and the chestnut and black frill that frames their white faces. Other waterfowl sometimes seen here include Musk Duck and Grey Teal.

Looking across to Susie Islet from the causeway, you might spy a Royal Spoonbill, a bird not often seen in Tasmania. Hoary-headed Grebes can also commonly be seen here.

## Kelp Gull
*Larus dominicanus*

Although the Kelp Gull was only discovered breeding in Tasmania during the mid 1950s, it has since increased its range, particularly in southern Tasmania. These fairly recent arrivals are more aggressive feeders than the endemic Pacific Gulls, and fears have been expressed that they are displacing the Pacific Gull.

Kelp Gulls breed mainly on small offshore islands, where they build bulky nests out of a variety of dried plant materials and seaweed.

On Orielton Lagoon, near the historic cemetery, Pacific Golden Plover and Red-necked Stint may be seen roosting on the rocks at the point. Both these birds breed in the Arctic and migrate to Tasmania for our summer. However, some of the immature Red-necked Stints over-winter here. Other migratory shorebirds seen on Orielton Lagoon include the Eastern Curlew, Sharp-tailed Sandpiper, Curlew Sandpiper and Common Greenshank.

Back on the main road into Sorell, turn right into Stores Lane, which leads to a bird sanctuary. Drive straight ahead down the lane to a small parking circle. From here, walk across to the mouth of the Sorell Rivulet where, at low tide, migratory shorebirds can be found feeding among the three species of gulls.

In the Lauderdale area, shorebirds move between a number of sites depending on variables such as water levels, tides and disturbances from dogs and humans. You'll need to explore several sites to maximise possibilities for seeing birds.

Just after Acton Road (C330) meets road B33, continue towards Lauderdale and you'll soon come to a small car park on the right, at the northern end of Ralphs Bay. Pied Oystercatchers are generally seen from here; it is estimated that up to 400 of them (or approximately 5 per cent of the Australian population of these birds) over-winter on Ralphs Bay. Due to its significance for migratory birds, Ralphs Bay is a designated conservation area that is listed on the Register of the National Estate.

Other birds to be seen here could include the Eastern Curlew, Greenshank, Red-necked Stint, Curlew Sandpiper (all species summer only), Double-banded Plover (winter) and Red-capped Plover (all year).

Unfortunately, as I write, an extremely disturbing development has been recently proposed for the northern part of Ralphs Bay—the most valuable part of the bay for migratory and resident shorebirds. The proposed development consists of a new village, yacht marina and waterfront parks which would be built on the mudflats of Ralphs Bay. If this appalling development proceeds it will completely destroy this vital area for migratory shorebirds. Hopefully, by the time this book is published this development will have been scrapped.

After driving along the spit at Lauderdale, turn left into Forest Hill Road and drive approximately 1 km to Clear Lagoon, which is on the left. While it may be dry, when the lagoon has water it is a good place for shorebirds. There is a gate for walkers to enter the site.

Returning to South Arm Road (B33), continue through Sandford, and turn left into Cremorne Avenue to reach the northern end of Pipe Clay Lagoon. Follow this to its end, then turn right so you can drive back along Pipe Clay Esplanade (unsealed) on the lagoon side of the road. High tide is best for observing birds here. Pacific, Kelp and Silver Gulls can all be

## Pacific Black Duck
*Anas superiliosa*

One of Tasmania's commonest waterfowl, the Pacific Black Duck is widely distributed across the state and may be found in a wide range of aquatic habitats such as rivers, lakes, coastal lagoons, swamps and farm dams, although they do prefer deep, freshwater swamps. The Pacific Black Duck is a typical surface feeder or dabbling duck and consumes a range of plant matter, such as seeds of water plants, as well as aquatic insects and crustaceans.

Most breeding occurs during spring, and the nest is typically a scrape in the ground in grass or reeds, lined with a considerable amount of down.

## Great Crested Grebe
*Podiceps cristatus*

The Great Crested Grebe is a very attractive bird with its dagger-like bill, double-horned crest and chestnut cheek frills. It is well known for its elaborate courtship display in which pairs dance on the water, head to head, and vigorously shake their fanned and raised head plumes. These grebes are frequently highly vocal, with loud, far-carrying calls.

Rare and nomadic in Tasmania, the Great Crested Grebe is sometimes seen at Orielton Lagoon, and once bred at Lake Dulverton when it was flooded. They may generally be seen on either side of the causeway between Midway Point and Sorell.

seen in their varying stages of maturity. Bar-tailed Godwits from the Arctic can be seen in summer, and other birds to watch for are Crested Tern, Pied Oystercatcher and White-bellied Sea-Eagle. Sooty Oystercatcher may be seen in winter.

Returning to the B33, to reach the southern end of Pipe Clay Lagoon, turn into Clifton Beach Road and follow this to Bicheno Street, then turn left and this will take you to the water's edge. When shorebirds such as Double-banded Plovers are here, they are best seen from the sealed section of the road. There is a small pull-off area for parking.

A little further along Bicheno Street (on the unsealed section), turn right to travel to Cape Deslacs. There is a gate at the car park, and from here it's about a two-minute walk to a viewing platform. Short-tailed Shearwaters can be seen here at dusk from September to May (except November).

Further south on the B33, you come to Calverts Lagoon. Park at the gate and walk the short distance to the lagoon. Birds you might see include Hooded and Red-capped Plovers, Pacific Black Duck, Chestnut Teal, Australasian Shoveler, Black Swan and Little Pied Cormorant. Black-winged Stilt (a vagrant to Tasmania) has also been seen here.

Heading further along road B33, there is a terrific lookout but, as it is poorly signposted, you'll have to watch to see the turn-off. It is marked with a sign saying 'South Arm Nature Recreation Area', but there are several such signs in the area. If you've descended the hill towards South

Arm, you've gone too far, so watch for it on your return journey. From the look-out there are terrific views to Betsey Island and Black Jack Rocks. Shy Albatross may be seen and, in the warmer months, Short-tailed Shearwaters can be seen grouped together in large 'rafts' as they feed.

At the narrow spit before South Arm, a number of migratory species can be seen feeding at low tide in summer, including Red-necked Stint and Curlew Sandpiper. Swamp Harriers are also often seen here.

While you're driving around this area, you may see Tasmanian Native-Hen and Masked Lapwing. There are plenty of Musk Lorikeets among the Blue Gums, and Australian Magpies are readily seen. If you're from Queensland or New South Wales, you will have noticed the white back of Australian Magpies here, rather than the black-backed variety you're used to. ▪

## Hooded Plover
*Thinornis rubricollis*

This stocky little plover is widespread around the coast of Tasmania, where it prefers ocean beaches and associated dune systems. Pairs return to traditional breeding territories during spring and the nest is a scrape in the sand. It is frequently placed against a beach-washed log, small plant or clump of seaweed.

Although remaining common this delightful plover is declining due to the increased use of beaches by four-wheel-drive vehicles, people, horses and dogs, which disturb nesting plovers and/or inadvertently destroy eggs or chicks. The Hooded Plover may be seen at Maria Island, Freycinet and South Bruny National Parks, as well as other east coast beaches.

# 22 Tinderbox Peninsula

Only 20 minutes south from Hobart, this peninsula is another excellent site for birdwatching, with several of Tasmania's endemic bird species easily seen. Most of the area is private property with hardly any reserves, although a quiet road extends around the peninsula, allowing for frequent stops to listen and look for birds. Adjacent to the south-east tip of Tinderbox Peninsula is Tinderbox Marine Reserve, which is a popular location for snorkellers and divers.

## Access

There are two main access routes. Firstly, from Hobart head south on the Southern Outlet (A6) towards Kingston. At the Kingston roundabout take the second exit, heading for Kettering. At the next roundabout take the second exit (Kettering) and continue for about 4 km. Take the first junction to the left, signed Howden. This road continues around Tinderbox peninsula.

The second option is to take the first exit from the second roundabout above. This road leads to Blackmans Bay. After 3 km, turn right onto Roslyn Avenue. This road continues around Tinderbox to meet the first access point.

## Facilities

On the south-eastern corner of the peninsula (about 6 km south of Blackmans Bay) is a small lookout at Piersons Point.

### EASTERN BARRED BANDICOOT
*Parameles gunnii*

Slightly smaller in size than the Southern Brown Bandicoot, this small marsupial (opposite) is also a more opportunistic feeder, eating insects, earthworms, bulbs, tubers and berries. This attractive bandicoot is instantly recognised by the three or four pale bands of fur across the hindquarters.

In Tasmania the Eastern Barred Bandicoot prefers areas of grassland interspersed with patches of scrub or woodland. It can be quite common in gardens close to areas of bush. Unfortunately, this delightful creature is suffering a population decrease in many areas due to large numbers of free-ranging dogs.

The Eastern Barred Bandicoot is sometimes seen at dusk around the picnic area at the entrance to Mt Field National Park or at Mt Nelson.

A small parking area and jetty can be found along the western side of the peninsula.

## Wildlife

This area is primarily of interest to birdwatchers, although the large dams and streams could hold Platypus. Other mammals to be found include Southern Brown and Eastern Barred Bandicoots, Common Brushtail and Common Ringtail Possums, and Tasmanian Bettong.

This bird haven holds a major population of Forty-spotted Pardalote. These tiny

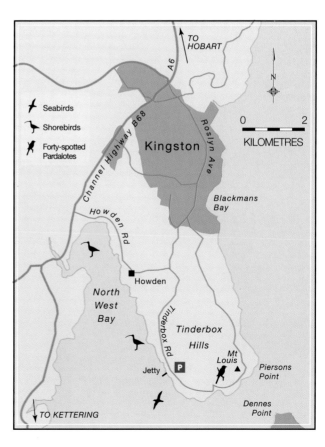

## Strong-billed Honeyeater
*Melithreptus validirostris*

The first indication of the presence of Strong-billed Honeyeaters is usually the sound of bark being torn from eucalypt trees. These endemic honeyeaters are gregarious birds which keep up a constant chattering while searching bark and crevices of trees for ants, weevils, beetles and spiders. They roam the forests in small flocks, frequently in company with Black-headed Honey-eaters.

Strong-billed Honeyeaters favour the taller, wetter forests and may be seen at Mt Field, Cradle Mountain–Lake St Clair and South Bruny National Parks as well as Mt Wellington.

## Eastern Spinebill
*Acanthorhynchus tenuirostris*

This small, colourful honeyeater frequently visits parks and gardens to feed on the blossoms of native and introduced plants. Eastern Spinebills have particularly long bills which have evolved to take advantage of deep-throated flowers such as correas and heaths.

Sometimes singly or in small loose groups, birds forage actively in heathland and the shrub layer of woodlands, where they may be seen hovering while feeding on blossom.

Eastern Spinebills breed mainly in late spring and summer and build a delicate cup nest of fine bark strips, grasses and moss, lined with hair and feathers, which is placed up to five metres above ground in a shrub or other dense foliage.

© Jim Napier

birds are generally to be found wherever Manna Gums occur. One regular site is the woodland on the slopes of Mt Louis on the opposite side of the road from the lookout at Piersons Point. It is also worthwhile looking closely at the foliage of other Manna Gums elsewhere on the peninsula as this endangered endemic could possibly be spotted in other areas.

Other birds to be seen should include most of the species listed for the nearby Peter Murrell Reserve. Wedge-tailed Eagle breeds in the Tinderbox area, and during summer fast-flying, noisy flocks of Swift Parrots may be seen. This rare and endangered parrot is particularly attracted to flowering eucalypts such as Blue Gum.

The scrub adjoining the jetty is a good area for birds and is not private property. This is also a good site for seabirds such as Black-faced Cormorant and Pacific, Kelp and Silver Gulls, as well as the White-faced Heron and Pied Oystercatcher in North West Bay.

Tasmania is a wonderful place to dive or snorkel and Tinderbox Marine Reserve offers a safe underwater experience to visitors of all ages. There is an abundance of fascinating marine life, including a large diversity of seaweeds, invertebrates and fish, including the beautiful Weedy Seadragon.

The waters here are shallow, sheltered and easily accessible so should not be missed.

## Black-faced Cormorant
*Phalacrocorax fuscescens*

Also known as the Black-faced Shag, this common and almost exclusively marine cormorant is able to excrete excess salt from its body by use of a nasal salt gland.

Black-faced Cormorants are frequently seen roosting on jetties, buoys or offshore rocks, and breed in small or large colonies on offshore stacks or islands. Nests are built of seaweed and leafy material and placed on the ground or on bare rock. Up to five eggs are laid although normally there are only three, and both sexes incubate the eggs.

This attractive cormorant may be seen at almost any coastal site listed in this book.

# 23 Tasman Peninsula

While usually linked to Port Arthur and its history, the Tasman Peninsula has some enthralling coastal landscapes. The Tasman National Park, which is just over 10,700 hectares in area, consists of three large separate parcels of land, as well as several smaller state reserves and historic sites. Extensive coastlines mean visitors are never far from the sea and can enjoy getting close to some sea-living wildlife. Several wildlife-watching boat tours operate from the Tasman Peninsula, offering added opportunities to enjoy seabirds, seals, dolphins and possibly whales.

Fees are required to enter some sections of the Tasman National Park.

Cape Hauy on the Tasman Peninsula is noted for its dramatic coastal scenery, including sheer cliffs, forested headlands and remote offshore islands.

The attractive She-oak Skink (opposite) has secretive habits and is rarely seen in the open. It is now known to be endemic to Tasmania and produces live young.

© Dennis Harding

## Access

Follow the Arthur Highway (A9) from Sorell, about 27 km north-east of Hobart. There are a number of ways to access the Tasman National Park and other reserves. Some key routes to sites of interest are outlined below.

The Tessellated Pavement and Pirates Bay are located at Eaglehawk Neck, about 56 km south-east of Sorell. Car parking and the access ways are well signposted.

The popular sites of the Blowhole, Tasman Arch and Devils Kitchen can be reached by road C338 from Eaglehawk Neck. A signposted gravel road leads from this road to Waterfall Bay. There is a walking track from the Devils Kitchen to Waterfall Bay. The Tasman Track is a four- to five-hour walk between Waterfall Bay and Fortescue Bay.

Midway between Taranna and Port Arthur, road C344 leaves the Arthur Highway and heads 12 km to Fortescue Bay. While unsealed, this road is suitable for two-wheel-drive vehicles. The road gives access to the Cape Pillar and Cape Hauy walking tracks and the southern end of the Tasman Track.

A signposted road, just north of Port Arthur, leads to Stewarts Bay.

Visiting Cape Raoul requires a five-hour return walk, on a track that is rough in sections. From Port Arthur take road B37 and drive 8 km west, then turn left at the sign to Highcroft and Stormlea, located at Parsons Bay Creek.

## Facilities

Public toilets are located at Eaglehawk Neck, the Blowhole, Fortescue Bay, Stewarts Bay, Port Arthur and Nubeena.

Fortescue Bay has campsites, picnic areas, drinking water and a boat ramp.

There are no facilities at the Cape Raoul car park or along the track, including no drinking water.

Food, fuel and accommodation are available at various places on the Tasman Peninsula, with Port Arthur and Nubeena the main centres.

For information about wildlife boat tours and bookings, contact the Tasmanian Visitor Information Network (see the White Pages).

## Wildlife

Good wildlife populations occur on the Tasman Peninsula; some quiet walking and watching at any of the reserved lands outlined above should have you seeing

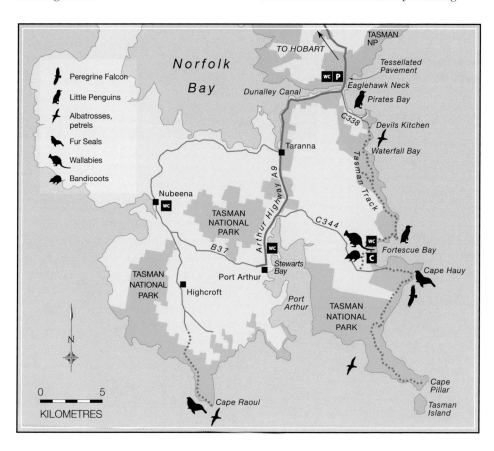

wildlife. As anywhere else, being out in the early morning and late evening will give you the best wildlife-watching opportunities.

Fortescue Bay has extensive bush camping areas that are good habitat for species such as Eastern Barred Bandicoot, Bennett's Wallaby, Tasmanian Pademelon and all four species of possum. The beach here has recorded very rich numbers of invertebrates such as crustaceans and sandhoppers, so it's no wonder mammals and birds are often seen foraging on it. Common Dolphins are sometimes seen in the bay, and Eastern Quoll might be seen scampering about the beach after dark.

Little Penguins come ashore at both Fortescue Bay and Pirates Bay. From Fortescue Bay you can walk out to Cape Hauy. At the end of the track, look far below to the base of the cliffs as this is a regular haul-out for Australian Fur Seals. Peregrine Falcons nest in the area and you could have one wheeling and screeching overhead, trying to scare you away from its territory.

If you walk to Cape Raoul, at the end of the track you can look down to the base of the cliffs at another popular area for Australian Fur Seals. A White-bellied Sea-Eagle is often seen above the lake near the end of this track.

The Dunalley Canal creates a barrier to the movement of land-based wildlife. To date, this has prevented the spread of Devil Facial Tumour Disease to the Forestier and Tasman Peninsulas, meaning Tasmanian Devils are in higher numbers in these areas. Technology is

## Australian Fur Seal
*Arctocephalus pusillus*

Although the Australian Fur Seal was formerly more abundant, it is still common around the islands and coast of Tasmania, as well as south-east Victoria and southern New South Wales. Large numbers typically haul out for breeding on exposed rocky islands, mainly in the Bass Strait. Fully mature males have massive necks and shoulders and dwarf the adult females.

Now fully protected, Australian Fur Seals may be seen by booking with a tourist boat operator on Bruny Island or on a cruise to Tenth Island from George Town on Tasmania's north coast. These two tourist ventures are the easiest way to view fur seals. Although fur seals do occur on offshore islands in the Furneaux Group, these islands are far more difficult to access and at present there are no organised boat tours.

## Peregrine Falcon

*Falco peregrinus*

One of the world's fastest birds, this powerful falcon is found throughout Tasmania in coastal or inland sites where there are suitable cliff ledges for nesting. It will attack and kill almost any bird that flies—even birds somewhat larger than itself. The Tasmanian falcon is larger than the mainland Australian falcon and unfortunately is frequently persecuted.

As well as in Tasman National Park, this spectacular raptor may be seen in Launceston's Cataract Gorge, on the Nut at Stanley, Maria Island and even in Hobart on the bridge over the Derwent River, where it often hunts starlings.

being developed to secure the Dunalley Canal bridge from being crossed by Tasmanian Devils and so maintain this quarantine zone.

If you're visiting the Port Arthur Historic Site, your admission fee will give access for 48 hours, and an evening stroll about the lawns and gardens is recommended. The site is lovely habitat for species such as Eastern Barred and Southern Brown Bandicoots and the Tasmanian Pademelon, as well as many bird species. The grounds are open until dark.

The chatter of feeding Swift Parrots makes their presence obvious. Good places to look for them in spring are the large Blue Gum trees at Fortescue Bay and Stewarts Bay.

On blustery days, the Devils Kitchen lookout is a good place to watch for petrels and albatrosses, as these birds fly closer to shore in rough seas. Albatross species that have been recorded by local birdwatchers on wildlife boat trips include the Black-browed, Bullers, Northern Royal, Yellow-nosed, Shy, Royal and Wandering Albatrosses. Petrel species observed include the Grey-backed, White-faced and Wilsons Storm-Petrels, and the Grey, Cape and Southern Giant Petrels.

Australasian Gannet, Crested Tern, Black-faced Cormorant, Short-tailed and Sooty Shearwater, Common Dolphin, Australian Fur Seal and Mako Shark have also been spotted. ■

# 24 Adventure Bay, the Neck and North Bruny

Bruny Island off the D'Entrecasteaux Channel is an absolute gem and should not be missed. From north to south, it extends to over 50 km and contains a large range of diverse habitats and some spectacular scenery. With so much to see it's probably best to allow several days to get the most from a visit.

Bruny is virtually two large islands joined by a long, narrow isthmus called the Neck. The northern area was once largely covered by dry sclerophyll woodland, although much has been cleared for farming. The southern part remains heavily forested, with patches of temperate rainforest on the slopes of Mt Mangana (571 metres).

## KEY SPECIES

- Southern Right Whale
- Little Penguin
- Short-tailed Shearwater
- White-bellied Sea-Eagle
- Tasmanian Native-Hen
- Hooded Plover
- Forty-spotted Pardalote
- Scrubtit

The spectacular Southern Right Whale is now increasing in numbers following protection and can frequently be seen in the sheltered bays of south-east and east Tasmania.

During the early European exploration of Australia, many famous explorers including Captain Cook, Captain Bligh, Admiral Bruny and D'Entrecasteaux all moored their ships in Adventure Bay on the east coast of South Bruny. Adventure Bay was named after Tobias Furneaux's ship, the *Adventure*, which anchored here in 1773.

This whole area is really superb for birdwatching.

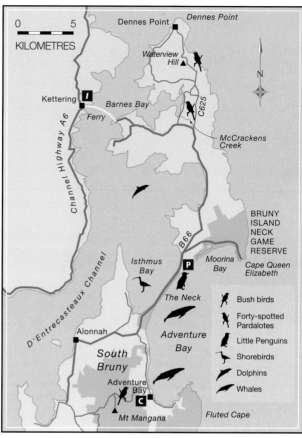

## Access

From Hobart take the Southern Outlet (A6) to Kettering, about a 40-minute drive or approximately 30 km. At Kettering, a ferry provides between nine and eleven crossings daily to Bruny Island (watch for fishing Australasian Gannets on the ferry crossing).

From the Bruny ferry terminal it is about 20 km to the Bruny Island Neck Game Reserve along the B66.

To get to the Neck and Adventure Bay, continue along the B66 from the ferry. After 7 km you will see a road to the left (C625). Turn right here (south) and continue on the B66 for another 13 km to the causeway across the Neck. Here there is a small car park on the left for Little Penguin viewing. To get to Adventure Bay, continue south across the Neck and then take the next road left, which leads to Adventure Bay.

## Facilities

Guest houses and rental accommodation are available on the island. There is a campsite at the southern end of the Neck with pit toilets. Adventure Bay has two caravan parks, a general store and fuel. There are also many car parks, picnic tables and walking trails on the island.

# Wildlife

## The Neck

At the start of the causeway on the isthmus you will see signs for the Little Penguin viewing area on the left of the road. You need to arrive here about 30 minutes before dusk and walk up to the small viewing platform. If you use a torch, cover the light with a piece of red cellophane. Please ensure that you only shine your torch onto the penguins once they have reached the vegetation. Never shine a light towards birds approaching from the sea across the sand, as they may turn around and head back out, leaving their chicks hungry in the burrows.

At dusk during summer you can experience the spectacle of thousands of Short-tailed Shearwaters returning to their burrows, followed by groups of Little Penguins that gather in the surf before clambering across the beach to their burrows in the dunes.

The diminutive Forty-spotted Pardalote is one of Tasmania's most sought-after birds and is restricted to areas of White or Manna Gums.

## Little Penguin
*Eudyptula minor*

Superbly adapted to a life at sea, the Little Penguin is able to 'fly' underwater due to its wings having been modified into flippers. The streamlined body is covered with thick down which underlies the short, stiff body feathers, and this provides excellent insulation while at sea.

The Little Penguin is the world's smallest penguin and the only one to breed in Australia or Tasmania. It waits until dark to come ashore; small groups gather in the surf before clambering across the beach or rocks to their burrows.

Little Penguins may be viewed at several recognised viewing sites in Tasmania including the Neck on Bruny Island, Bicheno, Burnie, Lillico Beach (near Devonport), Low Head (just north of George Town at the mouth of the Tamar River) (guided tour) and at Stanley.

## Short-tailed Shearwater
*Puffinis tenuirostris*

One of Tasmania's commonest birds, the Short-tailed Shearwater or Muttonbird breeds in huge numbers on many Bass Strait Islands as well as coastal mainland Tasmania.

At the end of the breeding season during autumn, Short-tailed Shearwaters depart on their migration to the north Pacific Ocean, and the adults return to their breeding colonies in Tasmania during September. The nest is a chamber lined with dead leaves at the end of a burrow up to 2 metres long.

Short-tailed Shearwaters may be viewed at several mainland Tasmanian sites such as the Neck on Bruny, Cape Deslacs (at South Arm), Ocean Beach at Strahan and Cressy Beach just south of Swansea.

The tidal bay to the west is worth scanning for oystercatchers and other birds such as Pacific Gull, Kelp Gull and Black-faced Cormorant.

About 2 km before the isthmus, a walking track leads to Moorina Bay and Cape Queen Elizabeth, passing several lagoons and patches of scrub. Birds seen here should include Swamp Harrier (summer only), Hooded Plover on the beaches and White-fronted Chat. Yellow-tailed Black-Cockatoos are frequently seen feeding in the coastal banksias.

**Adventure Bay**
This small historic village is the main holiday centre for Bruny.

Although Southern Right Whales were decimated by the whaling industry early last century, due to protection they are now recovering and Adventure Bay is one of their more regular sites. Southern Right Whales are migratory and arrive in the shallow bays of southern Australia and Tasmania to give birth to their calves during August to November. To check on recent sightings, ask the locals at Adventure Bay or contact the Parks and Wildlife Service.

Behind Adventure Bay village you may be lucky to spot one of the local white Bennett's Wallabies, which are fairly common here and appear to be spreading.

A large number of bird species may be seen here including the Purple Swamphen, Tasmanian

Native-Hen, White-faced Heron, Masked Lapwing, Hooded and Red-capped Plovers, Pacific, Kelp and Silver Gulls, Caspian and Crested Terns, Yellow-tailed Black-Cockatoo, Green Rosella, Swift Parrot (summer only), Pallid and Fan-tailed Cuckoos (summer only), Golden Whistler, Satin Flycatcher (summer only), Grey Shrike-Thrush, Grey Fantail, Superb Fairy-Wren, White-browed Scrubwren, Brown Thornbill, Yellow Wattlebird, Eastern Spinebill, Silvereye, Spotted Pardalote, Dusky Woodswallow (summer only), Beautiful Firetail, Forest Raven, Black Currawong, Dusky Robin, and honeyeaters such as the Black-headed, Strong-billed, Yellow-throated, Crescent and New Holland.

It is worthwhile driving up the Mt Mangana road, which although unsealed passes through areas of wet sclerophyll forest. A walking track leads to the top of Mt Mangana, passing through patches of temperate rainforest with Myrtle Beech, Blackwood, Leatherwood, Sassafras and Celery-top Pine. Although the rainforest holds few birds, you could see Tasmanian Thornbill, Pink Robin, Olive Whistler, Crescent Honeyeater, Bassian Thrush and Black Currawong. Look out for the cryptic endemic Scrubtit in wet fern gullies.

From Adventure Bay an interesting walking track heads out to Fluted Cape, skirting East Cove through dry forest which is excellent for birds. The island just offshore from the cape has breeding Little Penguins, and Pacific Gulls and Kelp Gulls are usually seen in the bay, together with Australasian Gannets fishing

© Jim Napier

## Scrubtit
*Acanthornis magnus*

The underbrush and thickets of wet sclerophyll and temperate rainforests are the preferred habitat of the Scrubtit, one of Tasmania's endemic bird species. This cryptic bird could easily be mistaken for a Scrubwren or a Thornbill, although the Scrubtit has a brown eye with a black centre, and a whitish eye-ring.

Being secretive and often solitary, the Scrubtit does need to be searched for. It spends most of its time foraging among the leaf litter and undergrowth, frequently ascending tree trunks while searching for insects, rather like a treecreeper.

Scrubtits are best looked for in damp forest areas at Mt Wellington and Mt Field National Parks and Lake St Clair.

## Tasmanian Thornbill

*Acanthiza ewingii*

Until fairly recently this Tasmanian endemic was considered to be another race of the Brown Thornbill. The Tasmanian Thornbill is, however, normally found in wetter habits such as rainforest and wet sclerophyll forests, where it forages through undergrowth and shrubberies for insects. The untidy dome nest of shredded bark, grasses and fragments of ferns are bound with cobweb and placed in the low branches of shrubberies or fern thickets.

You may see Tasmanian Thornbills at Mt Field and Maria Island National Parks as well as Mt Wellington and South Bruny.

offshore. There is also the chance here of seeing a White-bellied Sea-Eagle soaring overhead.

### North Bruny

Although North Bruny does not support the bird diversity that is found on South Bruny, it does hold a major population of Forty-spotted Pardalotes.

After leaving the ferry, drive for approximately 5 km, then turn left onto the Barnes Bay Road. After almost 2 km you reach a sharp left-hand bend where the road crosses a creek. This is McCrackens Creek. On the roadside are some large Manna Gums, *Eucalyptus viminalis*. Forty-spotted Pardalotes can usually be seen feeding in the foliage of these trees.

To see more Forty-spotted Pardalotes, continue north to Barnes Bay and head north-east on the Barnes Bay Road. After about 1 km you reach the Bruny Island main road. Turn left. Then after about 3 km you pass a wooded hillside. This is Waterview Hill, where a population of Forty-spotted Pardalotes resides. This rare and endangered endemic bird can usually be found feeding in the foliage of the Manna Gums which dominate the woodland on either side of the road. ■

© Jim Napier

© Rob Blakers

# 25 South Bruny National Park

Islands are usually perceived as attractive, romantic places and Bruny Island, with its wonderful coastal scenery, abundant wildlife, fascinating history and laid-back lifestyle, lives up to these notions. Cloudy Bay and the Labillardiere Peninsula are part of the South Bruny National Park. Labillardiere Peninsula takes its name from a French naturalist on the D'Entrecasteaux expedition, so you are following in historic footsteps as you do your own nature exploring.

## KEY SPECIES

- Echidna
- Australian Fur Seal
- Shy Albatross
- Ground Parrot
- Forty-spotted Pardalote
- Tawny-crowned Honeyeater
- Yellow-throated Honeyeater
- Beautiful Firetail
- Dusky Robin

## Access

Take the Southern Outlet (A6) from Hobart to Kettering, which is about 30 km or a 40-minute drive. A ferry at Kettering departs at regular intervals, making the 15-minute crossing to Bruny Island nine to eleven times daily. In busy periods, there are sometimes more cars wanting to travel than ferry space available, so it's best to arrive early. Bookings cannot be made in advance.

### Cloudy Bay

The most direct route from the ferry terminal is south via Alonnah and Lunawanna by road B66, then road C644 to Cloudy Bay. You can also travel from Adventure Bay on the east side of the island via road C629.

### Labillardiere Peninsula

Travel via road B66 to Lunawanna, then road C629 towards Cape Bruny. Just before Cape Bruny, a sign marks access to the Peninsula Walking Track. Take this road to its end at the Jetty Beach campsite. It takes about an hour and a quarter to drive from here to return direct to the ferry.

## Facilities

Cloudy Bay and Labillardiere Peninsula are 'out of the way', so arrive equipped with adequate fuel, food, water and any supplies you might need.

Small shops on South Bruny are located at Adventure Bay, where fuel can be purchased, and Lunawanna. There are two campgrounds at Adventure Bay, and a range of other accommodation scattered

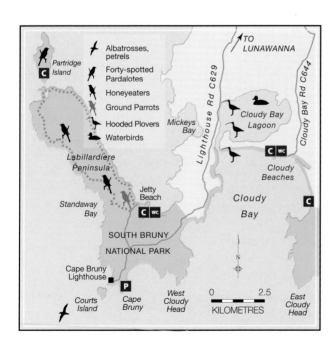

about the island. Bookings are best made in advance in the summer period.

There are four bush camping areas in South Bruny National Park, located at Cloudy Bay Road (just inland of Cloudy Beaches), Cloudy Corner (access is by a 3-km drive along Cloudy Beaches), Labillardiere Peninsula (Jetty Beach) and Partridge Island. Facilities are basic and there is generally no drinking water. Pit toilets are located at all four campsites and at the Cloudy Bay Road car park. Fireplaces (BYO firewood) are provided at all campsites except Cloudy Corner, which is a fuel-stove-only area.

There is beach access for boat launching at Cloudy Bay and Jetty Beach, and a jetty at Partridge Island (but mooring is not permitted).

There are some very good wildlife-watching tours on Bruny Island, both on land and offshore. For information and bookings, phone the Tasmanian Visitor Information Network on (03) 6267 4494, or call into the visitor centre beside the ferry terminal at Kettering.

## Wildlife

Bruny Island is typical of smaller islands in having a lower diversity of wildlife. The Tasmanian Devil, Common Wombat and Spotted-tailed Quoll do not occur on Bruny Island.

### Black-headed Honeyeater
*Melithreptus affinis*

An endemic honeyeater, the Black-headed Honeyeater often joins in flocks with Strong-billed Honeyeaters. The Black-headed Honeyeater has a completely black head and throat, with a pale blue crescent over the eye. These gregarious honeyeaters are noisy and active feeders and spend most of their time foraging among the foliage of eucalypts for ants, flies, beetles, spiders and honeydew.

They prefer the more open, dry forests of the lowlands and are therefore more common in the north and east of the state. Black-headed Honeyeaters may be seen at Mt Wellington, Maria Island and Mt Field National Parks, and Bruny Island.

## Dusky Robin
*Melanodryas vittata*

This endemic Tasmanian robin is a common and familiar bird across much of Tasmania and the Bass Strait Islands, inhabiting a wide range of habitats. It feeds by perching motionless on stumps or bare twigs before diving onto its prey of worms, beetles, flies or spiders. The nest is a loose cup of small roots and bark strips, bound together with cobweb and placed in a bush or in the hollow of a burnt-out stump.

Dusky Robins may be seen in almost any wooded habitat in Tasmania, and should be easily seen at Melaleuca Inlet, Bruny Island or the Peter Murrell Reserve.

Eastern Quolls do occur in good numbers, although it is uncertain whether this species is native to Bruny or whether it was introduced from mainland Tasmania. Tasmanian Pademelon and Brushtail Possum are all found in good numbers and can readily be observed. Common Brushtail Possums are known to occur in several colour phases, and Bruny is an area where the beautiful golden-haired variety is common, particularly in the Adventure Bay area.

Birdlife is prolific, with 140 species recorded on the island. All of the twelve Tasmanian endemic bird species occur in the South Bruny National Park.

The Forty-spotted Pardalote is perhaps the hardest endemic bird to locate, being very low in numbers and limited in habitat. If you're familiar with both *Eucalyptus viminalis* (White or Manna Gum) and the call of the bird from a recording, you'll improve your chances of finding it. Local bird-watching guides know how to find the pardalote easily as its habits are very regular. Being endangered, this little bird needs all the friends it can get, so perhaps you might like to spend a few hours with a local guide to ensure seeing it.

Large numbers of Australian Fur Seals frequent the waters off Cloudy Bay, with an estimated 800 seals using the Friars (a group of small islands just south of Tasman Head) as a haul-out. Seals are sometimes seen on Cloudy Beaches, but a boat tour should give some very good sightings.

The walking track around Labillardiere Peninsula passes through a wide variety of habitats, with tall eucalypt forest on the eastern side and heathland on the west. From the western side of the peninsula, there are terrific views of the Southern Ranges across the D'Entrecasteaux Channel. There are two beaches where Hooded Plovers and Pied Oystercatchers are usually seen. In the heathlands you might see Tawny-crowned Honeyeater, while Crescent and New

## Echidna
*Tachyglossus aculeatus*

Tasmanian Echidnas differ from the mainland form in having fewer spines and far more fur, but both are Short-beaked Echidnas. Only three mono-treme species occur worldwide, two in Australia and one (the Long-beaked Echidna) being found in New Guinea.

Although Echidnas are usually active during early morning or late afternoon, they are often found throughout the day during the cooler winter months. Tasmanian Echidnas breed from late winter to spring, and females lay a soft-shelled egg directly into their pouch.

Echidnas are more often to be encountered in the drier areas of the state, such as Mt William or Freycinet National Parks.

## New Holland Honeyeater
*Phylidonyris novaehollandiae*

The New Holland Honeyeater is a common bird of forests, scrub and heathland as well as parks and gardens. This attractively marked bird feeds almost exclusively on nectar from the blossom of shrubs and trees, although some small insects are also consumed.

After breeding at the end of summer, New Holland Honeyeaters gather into family parties or small loose flocks to forage and disperse across the countryside.

Holland Honeyeaters will be very obvious. In the forests on the eastern side of the peninsula, Strong-billed, Black-headed and Yellow-throated Honeyeaters, Beautiful Firetail and Dusky Robin can all be seen. The walk can be completed in a leisurely five hours, and is really terrific for bird-watching.

Besides birds, you can expect to see Echidnas and any of the three species of Tasmanian snakes, particularly during the summer months. The tracks are generally quite wide so there's plenty of space for humans and snakes to pass comfortably.

If you're camping at Jetty Beach you could wander out into the heathland at dawn or dusk and perhaps hear the chiming calls of a Ground Parrot.

Nearby, the Cape Bruny Lighthouse is worth a visit, especially in rough weather when albatrosses and petrels fly closer to the coast and may perhaps be seen from this exposed site. A White-bellied Sea-Eagle may also be seen soaring here. ■

*The*
# SOUTH-WEST

# 26 Melaleuca Inlet, Port Davey

Melaleuca Inlet is part of the vast Southwest National Park and Tasmanian Wilderness World Heritage Area that covers an area of approximately 440,000 hectares. Port Davey, Bathurst Harbour and Melaleuca Inlet are in fact a drowned river valley that was inundated around 6000 years ago when sea levels rose due to post-glacial melting. The marine environment is biologically unique and harbours relic aquatic organisms from over 80 million years ago.

This is a very remote area with a frequently harsh climate, so visitors to the region do need to be well prepared. Being surrounded by true wilderness, Melaleuca Inlet is virtually inaccessible except by light aircraft from Hobart. No roads, no shops and no hotels make visiting the region a true adventure. The only accommodation at Melaleuca consists of two huts that are provided for bushwalkers and other visitors.

Despite the difficulties inherent in visiting the area, Melaleuca Inlet is a paradise for bushwalkers and birdwatchers, with a wealth of breathtaking scenery. It is a prime site for wildlife, particularly birds— including Australia's rarest bird, the Orange-bellied Parrot.

## Access

Being surrounded by a designated wilderness area there are no roads, so visitors must either walk in or fly by light aircraft from Hobart. Walking involves carrying a rucksack and being completely

The Tasmanian Tree Frog, an attractive, large frog, is restricted to Tasmania where it is common in western mountain districts such as Cradle Valley and Mt Field as well as at Melaleuca.

Although Ground Parrots prefer to run from danger, they are strong fliers that are able to re-colonise areas of regenerating habitat following burning.

self-sufficient for a walk that takes from four to seven days through remote country.

Light aircraft fly regularly from the Cambridge airfield on Hobart's eastern shore. The flight takes approximately 45 minutes.

## Facilities

Accommodation is limited to two huts containing bunk beds that sleep up to ten persons per hut. Visitors intending to stay overnight must carry a sleeping bag, fuel stove and food for the duration of their stay.

Otherwise there is a small sheltered camping ground, a gravel airstrip suitable for light aircraft, a toilet and a ranger station, which may or may not be staffed.

A public hide has been built overlooking an artificial feeding area for Orange-bellied Parrots.

## Wildlife

The area of Buttongrass moorland, Tea-Tree scrub and woodland near the airstrip and surrounding the walkers' huts is a haven for birds and mammals. However, it is best to visit during spring or summer to coincide with the influx of summer migrants.

Be careful when walking around though, as Tiger Snakes are common and often bask on walking tracks.

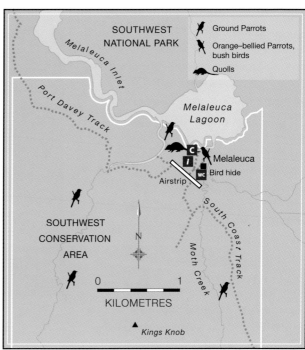

Close to the airstrip is a public hide overlooking a feeding station which has been built to allow close-up views of Orange-bellied Parrots—Australia's rarest bird, which numbers at best 200 individuals. The endangered Orange-bellied Parrot is a small but exquisite parrot that breeds only in south-west Tasmania and migrates during autumn to coastal areas on the south-east mainland.

During the last century the Orange-bellied Parrot population numbered in the thousands, but since then the population has declined drastically due to a variety of factors. Research has shown that the Orange-bellied Parrot nests in tree hollows in patches of woodland surrounding the Buttongrass moorland and feeds on seeds of small flowering plants growing on the plains. For thousands of years the Buttongrass moorlands were burnt on a regular basis by the local Aborigines to provide suitable habitat for wombats, Bennett's Wallabies and Tasmanian Pademelons, which provided the local inhabitants with a major source of food. This also allowed the local inhabitants to travel more easily through the bush.

However, following the forced removal of the Aborigines from the south-west, 'fire-stick farming' was no longer carried out, except by the few tin miners who moved into the area. If Buttongrass moorlands are not burnt on a regular basis, the vegetation very soon becomes long and dense and allows Tea-Tree scrub to proliferate, smothering the Orange-bellied Parrots' small flowering food plants such as Helichrysum Daisies and small boronias, thus obliterating the parrots' food supply.

Fortunately a program of controlled burning should now ensure a continued food supply for the Orange-bellied Parrots, at least at their breeding grounds.

This area is also a stronghold for the Ground Parrot which inhabits the Buttongrass moorlands. This is a very difficult bird to see, although they are sometimes flushed from the sides of walking tracks. The Ground Parrot is largely nocturnal and

## Eastern Quoll
*Dasyurus viverrinus*

Less arboreal and smaller than the Spotted-tailed Quoll, the Eastern Quoll occurs in two colour variations, the usual being fawn to grey with white spots, and the other black with white spots. Eastern Quolls inhabit a wide range of habitats from sea level to alpine country. They prey on a variety of animals from invertebrates to small mammals, birds and also fruit.

Although remaining widespread in Tasmania, the Eastern Quoll is likely to suffer a huge population decrease if foxes become established. It is most easily seen at Cradle Mountain–Lake St Clair and Mt Field National Parks.

## Orange-bellied Parrot
*Neophema chrysogaster*

On the brink of extinction, the critically endangered Orange-bellied Parrot is now restricted to approximately 200 individuals, making this diminutive gem possibly Australia's rarest bird.

Orange-bellied Parrots breed only in coastal south-west wilderness areas of Tasmania. Here their preferred habitat is the poorly drained Buttongrass moorlands, surrounded by patches of forest where they nest in holes in eucalypt trees.

The surest place to see an Orange-bellied Parrot in the wild is at Melaleuca Inlet where there is a public hide overlooking a feeding station. Orange-bellied Parrots are present there from November to March.

announces its presence by calling—mainly at dusk, but also at dawn. The call consists of a series of clear, bell-like, rising notes, which are used by ornithologists to census populations, and by the birds to advertise their territory.

Another inhabitant of the plains is the Southern Emu-Wren, which may be seen in family parties, sometimes climbing exposed stems of Buttongrass or sedges. Patches of Tea-Tree or Melaleuca scrub are likely to hold Striated Field-Wren (*Calamanthus*), Yellow-throated, New Holland and Crescent Honeyeaters, Olive Whistler, Beautiful Firetail, and Dusky and Pink Robins. In patches of woodland you can find Green Rosella, Sulphur-crested Cockatoo, Grey Shrike-Thrush, Bassian Thrush, Scrubtit, Tasmanian Thornbill, Tasmanian Scrubwren and Black Currawong.

Mammals include Spotted-tailed and Eastern Quolls (often foraging near the walkers' huts at night), Common Wombat, Bennett's Wallaby, Tasmanian Pademelon and Common Ringtail Possum. Smaller mammals include the Little Pygmy-Possum, Swamp Rat, Broad-toothed Mouse and Long-tailed Mouse.

Spotlighting at night, particularly in the vicinity of the walkers' huts, can be very productive if you want to see mammals. Listen for the soft, high-pitched twittering call of Ringtail Possums from patches of Tea-Tree scrub.

The small holes that cover the Button-grass moorlands are the burrows of Burrowing Crayfish, which form a major food source for local quolls. If you sit and wait quietly you may see a crayfish appear at the entrance to its burrow.

An interesting endemic frog, Burrow's or the Tasmanian Tree Frog, inhabits small pools in this area. This large and beautiful frog (the males are bright green) can often be located by its loud, duck-like quacking during summer.

Melaleuca Inlet is also well known as the former home of one of Tasmania's most famous bushmen, Deny King. This former tin miner and bird-lover created a home for his family on the banks of Moth Creek, which runs into Melaleuca Inlet. Deny's love for the wilderness and for birds in particular earned him the respect of many visitors, and his home at Melaleuca was always an open house for visiting fishermen, bushwalkers and naturalists.

His home was also an open house for the birds in his garden, which were attracted into the kitchen with whole cheeses and bowls of sugar. Several of the images in this book were captured in Deny's garden and would not have been possible without his help.

I will always cherish fondly my memories of adventures at Melaleuca with Deny, other friends and the wildlife.

Deny's house is still regularly used by his family. Please ensure their privacy is respected by not treating the house as a tourist venue.

## Long-tailed Mouse
*Pseudomys higginsi*

This attractive small placental mouse is endemic to Tasmania, where it remains common in the higher rainfall areas of western Tasmania. It is also found in wetter forests of eastern Tasmania as well as alpine country.

Although the Long-tailed Mouse is largely nocturnal it is sometimes seen during the day, particularly during winter. It is difficult to see in the wild unless spotlighting is tried, although it is a regular visitor to bushwalkers' huts to forage for scraps. It feeds on a range of fungi, fruit, seeds, insects and spiders.

The Long-tailed Mouse is sometimes seen at Melaleuca and in the huts on the Overland Track between Cradle Mountain and Lake St Clair.

# 27 Mt Field National Park

## KEY SPECIES

- Platypus
- Eastern Quoll
- Eastern Barred Bandicoot
- Superb Lyrebird
- Pink Robin
- Scrubtit
- Black Currawong

This is one of Tasmania's best-known national parks, covering an area of approximately 17,000 hectares. It protects a wide range of habitats and vegetation types including dense, tall forests of Swamp Gum, important areas of rainforest and scrub, and the shrublands, bogs and tarns of the alpine zone.

Mt Field was declared a national park in 1916 and along with Freycinet it shares the distinction of being Tasmania's first national park. Unfortunately, much of the original national park was revoked to allow for the clearing of forests for the timber industry.

Mt Field National Park offers the naturalist an incredible abundance of native plants as well as a diverse range of exciting and visible wildlife.

# Access

From Hobart take the Brooker Highway (A10) north-west to New Norfolk, following the Derwent River upstream. From New Norfolk take the A10 or B62 (either side of the river) to Westerway. From here, continue to the village of National Park, where the entrance to Mt Field is clearly marked. Mt Field is just over one hour's drive (about 75 km) from Hobart.

Although often difficult to spot, due to its small size, the Platypus is quite common across most of Tasmania even in farm dams.

# Facilities

Just outside the park entrance is a hotel; a variety of other accommodation exists in the area.

There are two main visitor areas in the park: one at the park entrance, and one at Lake Dobson.

The park entrance area has a visitor centre with shop and cafe, a caravan park and campground, and picnic facilities including electric barbecues and cooking shelters. There are also nature walks, including to the nearby magnificent Russell Falls where there is a peaceful walk beside the river.

At Lake Dobson there are cabins for rent offering basic accommodation. There is also a public shelter with tables, a wood-heater and toilet.

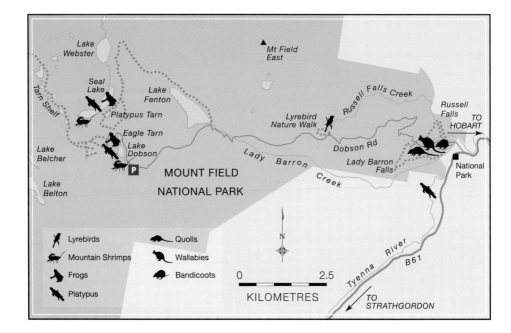

# Wildlife

Mt Field is an excellent area for viewing a variety of native mammals. Although most are largely nocturnal, some species do come out during late afternoon and are tame due to lack of persecution.

Bennett's Wallaby and Tasmanian Pademelon are both common around the campground and venture out in the late afternoon to graze in the picnic areas.

Also seen here are Southern Brown and Eastern Barred Bandicoots, and Brushtail Possum. Long-nosed Potoroo are common in Mt Field, although they do prefer dense undergrowth.

The Common Wombat is indeed common throughout the park, and if you are very fortunate you may also see an Eastern Quoll or even a Tasmanian Devil or Spotted-tailed Quoll.

The Tasmanian Tiger or Thylacine, now almost certainly extinct, once inhabited the Mt Field area. The last Thylacine to be put on public show was trapped in nearby Florentine Valley in 1933 and was exhibited at Hobart Zoo until it died.

Both the Platypus and Echidna are found at Mt Field, and this area is probably one of Tasmania's best sites for viewing the former. Platypus inhabit the Tyenna River near the park entrance and may be seen by sitting quietly near a slow-moving section of river during early morning or late afternoon. Platypus also inhabit the high alpine country where, during winter, their tracks are frequently seen crossing snow-covered tarns.

Other mammals found in the park include the Common Ringtail Possum, Eastern Pygmy-Possum and Little Pygmy-

Possum, Broad-toothed Mouse, Swamp Rat and the endemic Long-tailed Mouse. The Water Rat—Tasmania's only aquatic rodent—also occurs, and may be recognised by its long, white-tipped tail.

The Mountain Shrimp has existed unchanged for at least 250 million years and is common in the streams and tarns of alpine areas.

All three species of Tasmanian snake occur at Mt Field. They are all venomous and strictly protected, so they are best avoided and not molested.

The Tasmanian Tree Frog and the Tasmanian Froglet are both common in the Lake Dobson area.

Although Mt Field does not boast a long list of bird species, most of the Tasmanian endemics may be seen. These include the Tasmanian Native-Hen, Green Rosella, Dusky Robin, Tasmanian Thornbill, Scrubtit, Black Currawong, and the Strong-billed, Black-headed and Yellow-throated Honeyeaters. Many of these may be seen around the campground, as well as the Fan-tailed Cuckoo, Welcome Swallow, Tree Martin and Black-faced Cuckoo-Shrike (all species summer only).

Other birds likely to be seen here include the Sulphur-crested Cockatoo, Flame Robin, Golden and Olive Whistlers, Grey Shrike-Thrush, Grey Fantail, Superb Fairy-Wren, Eastern Spinebill, Spotted and Striated Pardalotes, Silvereye and Forest Raven.

One of the prettiest short walks for which Mt Field is well known is the Russell Falls Nature Walk. Although birds are not particularly numerous here, the

## Southern Brown Bandicoot
*Isoodon obesulus*

This rabbit-sized mammal requires areas of low groundcover which are periodically burnt. Their presence is normally recognised by a series of shallow conical holes in the soil, which have been dug with the powerful front claws while searching for earthworms or other invertebrates.

This nocturnal creature is sometimes seen in the vicinity of picnic or camping areas where they forage for scraps. The Southern Brown Bandicoot remains common throughout Tasmania, including agricultural areas, wherever suitable habitat remains.

## Little Pygmy-Possum
*Cercartetus lepidus*

The smallest of all Tasmanian possums is found across most of Tasmania, except parts of the far west. Like the Eastern Pygmy-Possum it undergoes periods of torpidity, particularly during winter when food is scarce. The Little Pygmy-Possum is largely insectivorous, feeding on a wide range of insects, spiders and small lizards.

Little is known of this minute creature's habits, due to its small size and secretive, nocturnal behaviour. This delightful animal is threatened through destruction of its nesting hollows by the firewood industry and clearing of old-growth forests.

many tree ferns are ideal habitat for Scrubtit, while Pink Robin is frequently seen near the falls. If you take a stroll here after dark, keep an eye out for the Glow Worms which are found here.

From Russell Falls it is possible to continue to Horseshoe and Lady Barron Falls through an area of wet sclerophyll forest. Birds to be found here could include the White Goshawk, Yellow-tailed Black-Cockatoo, Swift Parrot, Brush Bronzewing, Shining Bronze-Cuckoo, Bassian Thrush, Dusky Robin, Olive Whistler, Tasmanian Thornbill, White-browed Scrubwren, Beautiful Firetail, and Strong-billed, Yellow-throated and Crescent Honeyeaters.

Another bird which is difficult to miss here is the Superb Lyrebird. This species was introduced in 1934 from Victoria, where it was feared the species might be lost due to predation by foxes, and has become well established. Although a shy bird, the Superb Lyrebird certainly does have charisma and may sometimes be seen raking over the leaf litter with its powerful claws while searching for food. It is more usual though to *hear* a Superb Lyrebird, being a renowned mimic able to emulate a huge variety of sounds including those of the Grey Shrike-Thrush and Yellow-tailed Black Cockatoo, as well as chainsaws and a camera's motor drive!

In the high alpine areas it may be possible to spot a Wedge-tailed Eagle soaring overhead.

## Sulphur-crested Cockatoo
*Cacatua galerita*

Although nowhere abundant in Tasmania, this large cockatoo is patchily distributed in southern and western forests. Another population is centred on the Epping area of the northern Midlands, where they can frequently be seen foraging in paddocks.

These raucous parrots are very popular as pets and are able to thrive in captivity, where they are frequently gentle and affectionate towards their owners.

A small population of this conspicuous bird is to be found near Melaleuca Inlet in the state's south-west.

## Superb Lyrebird
*Menura novaehollandiae*

This largest of all songbirds has fascinated and enthralled naturalists since the beginning of European settlement. The long, shimmering train of the male is made up of sixteen highly modified tail feathers that play an important role during courtship displays. The spectacular courtship behaviour takes place on the display mound, which is built up by the male by scratching away vegetation with its long, powerful claws. Each individual male may make as many as twenty display mounds, although only a few will be used during the breeding season.

The Superb Lyrebird was introduced into Tasmania between 1934 and 1950 and is now well established and still spreading. These birds may be seen in the Hastings Caves area (at the southern end of the Huon Highway, south-west of Hobart) and Mt Field National Park.

179

# 28

# Lake St Clair

- Platypus
- Tasmanian Devil
- Eastern Quoll
- Bennett's Wallaby
- Tasmanian Pademelon
- Yellow-tailed Black-Cockatoo
- Scrubtit
- Black Currawong
- White-lipped Snake

Lake St Clair is the southern access point to the world-famous Cradle Mountain–Lake St Clair National Park. With an elevation roughly 200 metres lower than Cradle Valley there are differences in habitat types, species and climate.

Lake St Clair is a large glacial lake approximately 15 km long and almost 200 metres deep. The diverse environments around Lake St Clair include dry eucalypt forest, wet eucalypt forest, rainforest, Buttongrass moorland and sub-alpine communities.

As with any of the sites in this book, the more time you spend here, the more wildlife you will see.

## Access

Lake St Clair is accessed from the town of Derwent Bridge on the Lyell Highway (A10). Derwent Bridge is 175 km (two and a half hours) north-west of Hobart, and 85 km

Although Tiger Snakes (above) are venomous, they are not normally aggressive towards humans. This large snake gives birth to live young and feeds on frogs, small mammals and birds.

The delightful Eastern Pygmy-Possum (oppsite) is slightly larger than its relative the Little Pygmy-Possum, and occurs in most wet forests and rainforested areas of Tasmania.

The Bennett's or Red-necked Wallaby (right) is one of the more easily seen large mammals, particularly near picnic areas or campgrounds in national parks.

(one and a half hours) east of Queenstown. From Derwent Bridge it is 5 km to Lake St Clair.

The Lyell Highway has many winding sections and can be subject to ice, snow and heavy rain at any time of the year. Wildlife also travels on the Lyell Highway and unfortunately you will see a lot of road-kill along this road. To help protect wildlife the recommended speed after dark is 55 km per hour.

You can also access Lake St Clair from Launceston via Deloraine, taking the Highland Lakes Road (A5) onto the Marlborough Road (B11), then the Lyell Highway to Derwent Bridge.

There is no public transport to Lake St Clair, but bushwalker transport services are available. For information and bookings contact the Tasmanian Visitor Information Network (see the White Pages).

## Facilities

As you'd expect, this major park is equipped with a wide range of facilities, including a visitor interpretation centre with bushwalking information, picnic areas, wheelchair-accessible toilets, a restaurant with limited grocery supplies, chalet and bunkhouse accommodation, and a camping area with a limited number of powered sites.

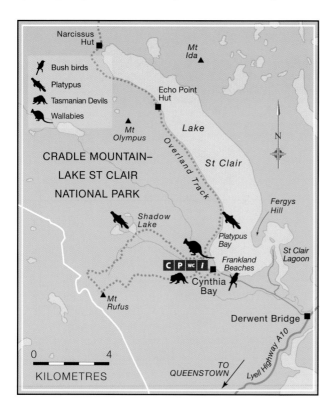

There are numerous walking tracks, as well as a ferry service on the lake.

Fuel and food are available at Derwent Bridge.

## Wildlife

There's wildlife to see here as soon as you arrive at the car park, and I'd be very surprised if the first local you met wasn't a Black Currawong. These birds with their beautiful metallic calls are a feature sound of the Tasmanian mountains. Other endemic birds you won't have to walk far to find are the Green Rosella and Yellow-throated Honeyeater. The latter is a beautiful bird and so easy to see here. If you've never had a good look at its vivid yellow-coloured throat, take the opportunity while you're here.

Bounding around are plenty of Bennett's Wallabies, often with a young joey in their pouch or at foot. Tasmanian Pademelons are usually not too far away either. If they are not apparent at first glance, have a look around the base of shrubby vegetation to find them. Tiger Snakes will be close by on warm summer days, so sensible footwear is a must.

The campground with its open parkland is a favourite wildlife-spotting area. Dusky Robin and Superb Fairy-Wren may be seen feeding in empty campsites, and the call of the Spotted Pardalote is often continuous here in spring and summer. The campground is a good place for

## Tawny Frogmouth
*Podargus strigoides*

The amazing camouflage of the Tawny Frogmouth makes it very difficult to spot in its daytime roost. Pairs mate for life and frequently roost together on a branch; at the slightest hint of danger they freeze and elongate their bodies to resemble a broken branch.

Tawny Frogmouths are strictly nocturnal and prey mainly on large nocturnal insects such as moths, as well as spiders and vertebrates. Their flimsy stick nest is built on the fork of a horizontal branch, where two pure-white eggs are laid.

To see a Tawny Frogmouth it is best to try spotlighting at night at any of the forested sites in northern or eastern Tasmania.

183

## Yellow-tailed Black-Cockatoo
*Calyptorhynchus funereus*

A flock of large, spectacular Yellow-tailed Black-Cockatoos flapping slowly over coastal scrub or inland woodland with far-carrying wailing cries is very much a feature of the Tasmanian bush. These large, noisy, nomadic parrots feed on wood-boring larvae of moths and beetles, as well as seeds of banksias and pine cones. They nest in hollows high in eucalypt trees and so are almost totally dependent on old-growth forests with suitable holes and cavities.

Yellow-tailed Black-Cockatoos may be seen at many of the sites in this book including Mt Wellington, the Neck on Bruny Island, and Mt Field, Freycinet, Mt William and Narawntapu National Parks.

after-dark prowls, when you might be lucky enough to see a Tasmanian Devil sniffing out the residues of campsite cooking. Southern Boobook Owls, with their 'more pork' call, are another regular night-time local.

After dark, Common Brushtail Possums often lurk around rubbish bins at the visitor centre and in the campground. With their distinctive high-pitched twittering call, Common Ringtail Possums are more often heard rather than seen. After dark, places to look for them are the trees around the main car park, and in trees between the visitor centre and the jetty. The lawns between the visitor centre and the lake are also worth an after-dark exploration.

The two monotremes, Echidna and Platypus, are both regularly seen here. Echidnas are most easily seen in the dry eucalypt forest, although places such as the Shadow Lake track, Larmairremener Tabelti Aboriginal cultural walk and even the beach beside Cynthia Bay are all regular haunts for this spiny mammal. With a little patience, you've got as good a chance of seeing a Platypus here as anywhere else in Tasmania. Early mornings and late evenings are best and quietness is essential. The Platypus Bay track gives some good vantage points to view regular Platypus locations.

A tiny little local that I've come across several times at both Cynthia Bay and Narcissus is the Eastern Pygmy-Possum. It's not highly obvious, but if you spot a tiny ball of fluff in a crevice in your cabin or other building, have a closer look.

The track to Echo Point and Narcissus passes mostly through rainforest. You could walk a short section of track and return, or catch the ferry to one of these places and walk back. There's plenty of evidence of Yellow-tailed Black-Cockatoos along the way in the form of shredded rotted logs that these large birds have torn apart to extract grubs. Another beautiful rainforest creature is the Macleay's Swallowtail—a large pale-green and black-coloured butterfly. It's almost always found near rainforest as the larvae feed on the leaves of Sassafras trees.

The Mt Rufus circuit track travels through a good mix of vegetation communities. The shady rainforest areas on the climb up are popular with Pink Robin and Tasmanian Scrubwren. Also here are Scrubtit, Brown Thornbill and Tasmanian Thornbill. It does take a keen eye and a knowledge of their calls to tell some of these birds apart.

Moving up the slope and into the more open forest, regulars include the Grey Shrike-Thrush, Crescent Honeyeater and Forest Raven. On the track you'll definitely notice the cube-shaped droppings of Common Wombats. These animals use their droppings to mark out territory, with tracks, rocks and fallen branches common sites for depositing.

There are usually plenty of small lizards to be seen, and the Ocellated Skink, Southern Snow Skink and Metallic Skink all occur here. You can often get quite close to these little lizards, so take a good look at their markings and you will soon start spotting the different species. The

## Grey Shrike-Thrush
*Colluricincla harmonica*

The powerful, melodious song of the Grey Shrike-Thrush is a familiar sound of the Tasmanian bush and may be heard from over half a kilometre away. The rich and beautiful call has given rise to the local name 'Joe Whiddy' and it is often mimicked by Superb Lyrebirds.

Grey Shrike-Thrushes are mostly carnivorous and catch a wide range of prey including lizards, insects, small mammals and nestlings as well as some carrion. It adapts well to human presence, even becoming quite tame if encouraged, and readily forages for scraps at picnic grounds. It is widespread across much of Tasmania, occurring in most wooded habitats including coastal scrub, parks and gardens.

This species is easily seen and quite tame at Melaleuca.

## Superb Fairy-Wren

*Malurus cyaneus*

One of south-east Australia's most popular birds, the Superb Fairy Wren is well known for the beauty of the male's iridescent breeding plumage and its jaunty, cocked tail. Non-breeding males, females and juveniles are mostly duller and brown-bodied, although adult males always have blue tails.

The Superb Fairy Wren has adapted well to suburban living and is regularly seen in parks and gardens as well as woodland, forest and scrub.

little pale-green to grey-coloured White-lipped Snake feeds exclusively on skinks, but you'll have to be quick to spot it as it will slither off as soon as it senses approaching footsteps.

Shadow Lake is another place where Platypus are often seen, and the tall eucalypt forests as you descend the track from here are good places for seeing birds of the open forest, such as Black-headed and Strong-billed Honeyeaters.

Swift Parrots are nomadic throughout Tasmania after about Christmas and, depending on the availability of blossoms, may be at Lake St Clair. I've seen them at Narcissus as late as April.

Don't forget to spend some time looking at the lake itself and wandering its shores around Cynthia Bay and the Frankland Beaches. Unfortunately its once extensive beaches are now underwater due to flooding of the lake in 1937. Tasmanian Native-Hens are often seen in grassy openings near the lake. There have also been recordings of the migratory Latham's Snipe in summer.

Seeing a Tasmanian Devil or a Spotted-tailed or Eastern Quoll is high on the list for many visitors. One way to increase your chances of seeing these animals is to go for a slow drive late at night. Suitable roads in this area include the road to St Clair Lagoon, the Rufus Weir Road and poking about the numerous other unsealed roads that leave from the Lyell Highway in the vicinity of Derwent Bridge. It's also possible to see a Tawny Frogmouth or a Southern Boobook Owl sitting on a roadside post. ▪

# 29

# Strahan and Macquarie Harbour

The small town of Strahan sits by the expansive waters of Macquarie Harbour on Tasmania's west coast. Strahan's history has many chapters that include the Huon Pine industry, a bustling port transporting the mineral riches of Queenstown, and the bitter conflicts of the Franklin River campaign. Today, fishing and tourism are the lifeblood of the town. Some locals have lived through it all, from rowing wooden boats across the harbour, having family disputes about damming the Franklin River to working on the modern tourist vessels that ply Macquarie Harbour today.

Despite its modernity, Strahan is only a breath away from the wild country that surrounds it, and wildlife-watching can be enjoyed quite close to the heart of town.

## KEY SPECIES

- Ground Parrot
- Orange-bellied Parrot
- Azure Kingfisher
- Southern Emu-Wren
- Dusky Robin
- Tasmanian Scrubwren

## Access

Strahan can be reached by the B24 from Queenstown, or by the B27 from Zeehan. For details regarding bus transport options contact the Tasmanian Visitor Information Network (see the White Pages). There are airports at both Strahan and Queenstown.

This exquisite male Orange-bellied Parrot displays brighter colours than the female. Note the deep-orange belly, the indigo leading-wing edges and blue frontal forehead band.

The swampy Buttongrass moorlands of western Tasmania are riddled with the small burrows of Burrowing Crayfish. These small crayfish are omnivorous and live on plant roots, algae, decaying and fresh Buttongrass and some worms and insects.

## Facilities

Food, fuel and accommodation can all be purchased in the town. However, Strahan's popularity means that all accommodation and restaurants are heavily booked in summer, so advance bookings are a must.

Queenstown and Zeehan could be alternative sources of accommodation, but these towns too are often booked out.

The many tour options for enjoying this famed area include cruise boats, float planes, canoe trips, jet boats, history plays and the ingenious Abt railway.

## Wildlife

A drive out of town west towards Ocean Beach will give you vistas of Buttongrass moorlands. While some describe these moorlands as monotonous, they are anything but. Over 165 species of flowering plants have been recorded in Buttongrass moorlands and they conceal a wealth of wildlife. In particular, the Buttongrass moorlands of south-west Tasmania are critical habitat for two rare, beautiful and somewhat elusive parrots.

The Orange-bellied Parrot is one of Australia's rarest birds and its migration route includes the Buttongrass moorlands of the west coast. This parrot breeds at remote Birchs Inlet on Macquarie Harbour, where there are no facilities and the only access is by charter boat from Strahan. If intending to visit, please contact the Parks and Wildlife Service in Strahan so they can advise the volunteer wardens at Birchs Inlet to expect you. The warden service operates from September to March and keen birdwatchers with remote-area living experience are welcome to apply (see www.wildcaretas.org.au). Birchs Inlet is also a prime site for Azure Kingfisher.

The Ground Parrot is a nocturnal bird that is generally heard rather than seen. In the right habitat this fascinating bird can easily be heard, usually at dawn or dusk. At Strahan, Ground Parrots can be heard in the Buttongrass moorlands in the vicinity of the airport, and this is possibly the premier site in Tasmania to see (or at least hear) this species. It's best to drive out before dusk, park the car and get settled

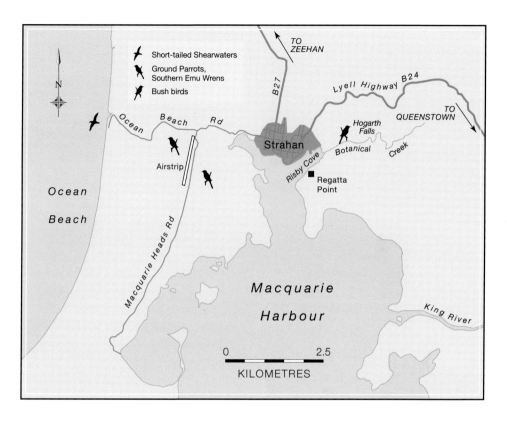

somewhere, either on the edge or a short distance into the Buttongrass moorland area. If you're unsure what Buttongrass is, you'll soon work it out: the tussocks of long, slender stems with button-shaped flower heads are pretty obvious to spot.

Once you've selected a place to listen for the parrots, it's best to keep quiet so as not to frighten any nearby birds. Ground Parrots call for about 30–40 minutes at dawn and dusk, and feed at night. It could be almost dark when you begin to hear birds calling; their call can be described as a series of high-pitched, bell-like notes. Like most birds, Ground Parrots have a range of calls. A series of sharper notes

on an ascending scale is a recognisable call of this bird.

The call of one bird will soon be followed by another calling back. If you're lucky, you might see a bird take flight in the fading light—and if you're *really* lucky you might see one of these predominantly green birds with black markings actually walk close by between the tussocks.

Another bird that you're very likely to see in the Buttongrass moorlands is the Southern Emu-Wren. This species is unmistakable as the male has a lovely powder-blue coloured throat, upper breast and brow.

Besides the endearing birds described

189

## Tasmanian Scrubwren
*Sericornis humilis*

Another of Tasmania's endemic birds, the Tasmanian Scrubwren is a small, dark-brown bird which is widespread and common in Tasmania. Its preferred habitats are the wetter forests, Tea-Tree thickets and densely vegetated gullies, where it spends most of its time foraging on the ground. It also frequently occurs in dense shrubberies of gardens, where it can become surprisingly tame.

Tasmanian Scrubwrens are frequently seen in groups that maintain contact with a harsh, staccato, buzzing call. They may be seen at Melaleuca, Mt Wellington, Mt Field and Cradle Mountain–Lake St Clair National Parks.

© Jim Napier

here, there's an array of other wildlife in the moorlands. Looking at the base of the tussocks you should probably see small tunnels made by other ground-dwellers such as the Broad-toothed Mouse.

You will note that muddy areas between the grass tussocks are pockmarked with small holes, mainly containing water. These are the burrows of Burrowing Crayfish, which are widespread here.

Also near the airport is Ocean Beach, where you can enjoy a wondrous sunset. As many visitors to Tasmania live in eastern Australia, watching a sunset is a rare treat. At Ocean Beach you can also enjoy the spectacle of Short-tailed Shearwaters returning to shore. There's a viewing platform in the colony where visitors can enjoy these birds without damaging the burrows.

In Strahan itself, you can walk along the foreshore and enjoy bush birds such as Dusky Robin, Grey Fantail and Tasmanian Scrubwren darting about in the Tea-Tree scrub, or perhaps watch cormorants, gulls and ducks amid the rustic vessels moored on Risby Cove. It's quite possible to see an Azure Kingfisher perched by the water. Those catching the Abt railway might also spot this bird by the King River.

From the Foreshore Walking Track you can access the Peoples Park and walk to Hogarth Falls. On an evening walk here, you could see Tasmanian Pademelon or Common Brushtail Possum, and there is always the possibility of seeing a Platypus in Botanical Creek. Regardless of what wildlife you see along the way, a walk to Hogarth Falls is always a pleasure.

## Ground Parrot
*Pezoporus wallicus*

One of the only three ground-living parrots in the world, the secretive Ground Parrot has its stronghold in western Tasmania. In Tasmania they are found in extensive and poorly drained Buttongrass moorlands and sedgelands, where they are largely nocturnal. They become active towards dusk, when they begin to call. The calling carries well on a still evening and consists of a series of thin, clear, ascending, bell-like notes.

The best hope of seeing or hearing a Ground Parrot is in the sedgelands surrounding Strahan airport or at Melaleuca.

## Grey Fantail
*Rhipidura fuliginosa*

The erratic twisting and turning flights of this small, long-tailed bird have earned it the local name of 'Cranky Fan'. These highly active aerial antics are in fact feeding forays, enabling Grey Fantails to catch a range of flying insects in midair.

Grey Fantails build amazing nests of plant fibres bound together with cobweb. These small cup nests are placed on top of a thin, horizontal fork of a branch up to six metres above ground level. They are common in most wooded habitats such as sclerophyll woodlands, coastal scrub and Tea-Tree-lined watercourses.

© Jim Napier

# Other wildlife sites

There are many other lesser sites in Tasmania that are of great interest to the wildlife enthusiast.

**Mole Creek Karst National Park**
This small national park in the mid-north of the state may be accessed via Mole Creek on the B12 road from Deloraine, due west of Launceston. The caves are well signposted from this road. More than 300 caves, sinkholes and underground streams are protected. Wildlife consists mainly of unique invertebrates such as Cave Crickets, Mountain Shrimps and Cave Spiders, together with a spectacular display of Glow Worms at Marakoopa Cave.
Contact  Mole Creek Caves Office, c/o Post Office, Mole Creek TAS 7304
Phone  61 3 6363 5182.

**Hastings Caves and Thermal Springs**
Hastings Cave State Reserve is reached via the Huon Highway (A6) and is about 125 km south of Hobart. This site is well signposted south of Geeveston. As well as Cave Crickets, this site is a regular for spotting a Platypus.
Contact  Hastings Caves, 754 Hastings Caves Rd, Hastings TAS 7109
Phone  61 3 6298 3209.

**Lillico Beach Little Penguin viewing area**
The Lillico Beach Conservation Area is located 6 km west of Devonport and is well signposted from the Bass Highway (A1). Little Penguins are active at dusk from October to March and can be seen from a public viewing platform. During holiday periods volunteer naturalists are available to assist.

## Wildlife parks
**Trowunna Wildlife Park**
PO Box 183, Mole Creek TAS 7304
Phone  61 3 6363 6162
Email  info@trowunna.com.au
Web  www.trowunna.com.au

**Bonorong Wildlife Park**
Briggs Rd, Brighton TAS 7030
Phone  61 3 6268 1184
Email  bonorong@bigpond.com

**East Coast Natureworld**
PO Box 105, Bicheno TAS 7215
Phone  61 3 6375 1311
Web  www.natureworld.com.au

**Something Wild Wildlife Sanctuary**
2082 Gordon River Road, National Park TAS 7140
Phone  61 3 6288 1013
Email  mail@somethingwild.com.au
Web  www.somethingwild.com.au

**Tasmanian Devil Conservation Park**
5990 Port Arthur Highway, Taranna TAS 7180
Phone  61 3 6250 3230
Web  www.tasmaniandevilpark.com

# Useful contacts

## Fox sightings
Please report any **fox** sightings to
the 24-hour hotline: 1300 369 688
(1300 FOX OUT)

## Devil and whale sightings
To report any **whale** strandings or
sightings, or if you see a **Tasmanian Devil**
with Devil Facial Tumour Disease, please
call the Wildlife Management Branch's
24-hour hotline: 61 3 6233 6556

## Conservation and wildlife
**Parks & Wildlife Service Tasmania**
GPO Box 1751
Hobart TAS 7001
Phone 1300 135 513
Web www.parks.tas.gov.au

**Birds Australia**
60 Leicester St
Carlton VIC 3053
Phone 1300 730 075
Email mail@birdsaustralia.com.au
Web www.birdsaustralia.com.au

**Birds Tasmania**
GPO Box 68
Hobart TAS 7001

**Fox Free Tasmania Taskforce**
PO Box 46
Kings Meadows TAS 7249
Email Fox.Enquiries@dpiw.tas.gov.au

**Tasmanian Conservation Trust**
102 Bathurst St
Hobart TAS 7000
Phone 61 3 6234 3552
Email tct@southcom.com.au
Web www.tct.org.au

**Wilderness Society**
GPO Box 716
Hobart TAS 7001
Phone 61 3 6270 1701
Email info@wilderness.org.au
Web www.wilderness.org.au

## Tourist information
**Tourism Tasmania**
GPO Box 399
Hobart TAS 7001
Phone 61 3 6230 8235
Email reception@tourism.tas.gov.au
Web www.discovertasmania.com
www.tastravel.com.au

**Aboriginal Land Council of Tasmania**
PO Box 386
North Hobart TAS 7002
Phone 61 3 6231 0288

## Tours and cruises

There are many eco-tour companies in Tasmania. However, as these businesses tend to come and go, here is a shortlist of several that we know can offer valuable wildlife-watching experiences.

Pelagic boat trips operate out of Eaglehawk Neck several times each year. For forthcoming trip details contact:
**Email** R.Clarke@zoo.latrobe.edu.au

**Arthur River Cruises**
Close-up views of White-bellied Sea-Eagles practically guaranteed.
1414 Arthur River Rd
Arthur River TAS 7330
**Phone** 61 3 6457 1158
**Web** www.arthurrivercruises.com

**Bruny Island Charters**
907 Adventure Bay Road
Adventure Bay TAS 7150
**Phone** 61 3 6293 1465
**Email** info@brunycharters.com.au
**Web** www.brunycharters.com.au

**Inala**
This group offers specialised, personalised fauna, flora and birding tours on Bruny Island, conducted by Dr Tonia Cochran.
**Web** www.inalabruny.com.au
**Email** inala@tassie.net.au
**Phone/fax** 61 3 6293 1217

**World Heritage Cruises**
Operates daily out of Strahan, travelling across Macquarie Harbour and up the Gordon River, landing visitors at the historic spot where blockaders mounted a protest against damming of the Franklin River, one of the world's few remaining truly wild rivers. Possible sightings of Azure Kingfisher.
**Web** www.worldheritagecruises.com.au

# Further information

## Books

Cameron, Mary (ed.), 1981, *A Guide to the Flowers and Plants of Tasmania*, Launceston Field Naturalists Club, Reed Books, Sydney.

Hutchinson, Mark, et al., 2001, *Snakes and Lizards of Tasmania*, Department of Primary Industries, Water and Environment Tasmania, Hobart.

Kirkpatrick, J.B. and Backhouse, Sue, 1989, *Native Trees of Tasmania*, Pandani Press, Hobart.

Ludeke, Michael, 2001, *Tasmania's Maria Island: A comprehensive history and visitors' guide*, Ludeke Publishing, Hobart.

McQuillan, Peter, 1994, *Butterflies of Tasmania*, Tasmanian Field Naturalists Club Inc., Hobart.

Mattingley, Christobel, 2001, *King of the Wilderness*, Text Publishing, Melbourne.

Plowman, Cathie, 2006, *The Overland Track: One walk, many journeys*, Parks & Wildlife Service Tasmania, Hobart.

Watts, Dave, 1993, *Tasmanian Mammals: A field guide*, Peregrine Press, Kettering, Tasmania.

Watts, Dave, 2002, *Field Guide to Tasmanian Birds*, New Holland, Sydney.

## Brochures

Parks & Wildlife Service, *Tasmania's Great Short Walks*, available from PWS offices

Birds Tasmania, *Endemic Birds of Tasmania*, a series of three brochures available from Birds Tasmania, GPO Box 68, Hobart TAS 7001

## CDs

*Frogs of Tasmania*, produced by the Central North Field Naturalists, available from Wilderness Society shops.

*Australian Birdcalls: Tasmania*, by David Stewart/Nature Sound Australia, available from Wilderness Society shops.

# Index

# Map key

| | | | |
|---|---|---|---|
| **P** Parking | Echidna | Dolphin | Raptor |
| **WC** Public toilets | Platypus | Seal | Bush bird |
| **i** Information | Bandicoot | Whale | Snake |
| **C** Camping | Kangaroo/wallaby | Native-Hen | Frog |
| National Park | Quoll | Waterbird | Crab |
| Rural Area | Tasmanian Devil | Penguin | Shrimp |
| Urban Area | Wombat | Seabird | |
| Walking Track | Mouse | Shorebird | |